INTOXICATING
Paris

*Uncorking the
Parisian Within*

PJ ADAMS

Photos by John Birkhead and Shutterstock with permission.

For information: www.pjadamsbooks.com

Intoxicating Paris: Uncorking the Parisian Within
Editor: Andrea Glass
Developmental Editor: Shaun Griffen

Copyright © 2013 PJ Adams
All rights reserved.

ISBN: 0989516202
ISBN-13: 9780989516204
ISBN (ePub): 978-0-9895162-1-1

Library of Congress Control Number: 2013910513
PJ Adams Books, San Clemente, CA

Manufactured in the United States of America

For Ashley, John, and Paris lovers everywhere

Contents

Introduction

J'adore Paris.

But I have to admit it's a prickly kind of love.

I admire the grand avenues, exquisite wines, and incomparable art in Paris. I adore her charming street *cafés* and her open-air *marchés* where anyone can buy a bit of *Comté* and a *baguette* for an impromptu picnic by the Seine. I certainly relish her expensive meals of *bœuf bourguignon* chased by a fine glass of *Château Latour* and finished off with a *mille-feuille* for dessert. They feel like sex on the tongue, but the pleasure lasts for hours and even longer in the memory, maturing like a fine wine to be savored over and over.

But then there are the pesky problems. Having to speak a little French or negotiate the French temperament that can turn in a flash from charm to pique. Remembering to employ French dining customs in order to ensure decent service. Or trying to squeeze my American body into a tiny French *robe* (dress).

Paris is frankly a beguiling, but eccentric lover—with a sometimes capricious bite.

Intoxicating Paris: Uncorking the Parisian Within explores what it's like to be an American psychotherapist in Paris, to move among the French, share their lifestyle, and understand a bit of how French people think, feel, love, and live out their lives. It's about negotiating life in Paris, discovering how to dine, what to tour, when to engage, where to shop, and frankly, how to love Parisians despite their mercurial nature.

In *Intoxicating Paris: Uncorking the Parisian Within* we'll get personal, delving into the French psyche to understand passion as only the French do it. We'll examine the French lifestyle from an American perspective to interpret a bit of how the French mind and willpower work. And we'll look at some of the differences between French men and French women and their American counterparts, as well as their attitudes toward home and country.

We'll also look closely at French parenting techniques and mine the secret to all those well-behaved French children. Deliciously, we'll also dissect how the ripening French woman maintains her allure (and her sex life), and we'll take a stroll through a French emergency room—from my personal experience.

We'll look at the world of shopping in the grand department stores, and also in some of the shops and boutiques along the byways. We'll discover how even an American can acquire some of that famous Parisian style without having to be a size *deux*. We'll travel through some of the street markets, examining the art of savvy buying from street vendors. And we'll uncover some conversational French phrases to assist visitors in France.

We'll visit *café* life and explore French cuisine like *blanquette de veau* and *bouillabaisse*, as well as the magic behind classic desserts like *macarons* and *ganache*. We'll discover why creativity flourishes in Paris, and how some of the world's most famous creators like Hemingway, Hugo, Rodin, Sartre, and Joyce found their genius there. Finally, we'll sift that special Parisian *joie de vivre*, the inspiring joy of life that drives her citizens and resonates in the 29 million+ yearly visitors who are lured by Paris's charms—and who are willing to put up with her idiosyncrasies.

From love to lingerie, coupling to parenting, Nicholas Sarkozy to James Bond, markets to medicine, and much more, I hope to entertain and enlighten. Done with humor and affection, I tip my beret to my exasperating, but beloved, Paris. I hope you enjoy reading *Intoxicating Paris: Uncorking the Parisian Within* as much as I enjoyed writing it. *Profitez de votre voyage* (Enjoy your journey). *Merci.*

Femininity

"What is it about French women that makes them so maddening...It's about luxe and calme mixed with just the right amount of volupté. And the worst of it is that French women seem to do all of this with an ineffable assurance which the rest of us can only dream of emulating but never perfecting. No wonder they drive us—and men—mad."

—Gulley Wells,
"Paris Underneath It All," *Conde Naste Traveler*

The French woman. She's truly unique in the world. Brazil has its beauties in bikinis. Italy has its raven-haired maidens. Even Scandinavia has its robust blondes. But the French female, with her pert figure, pouty lips, and irresistible *panache* is without peer.

The French woman—on the street, in a *café*, or in the *métro*—has an assured sense of self that is palpable. In fact, there's a French phrase that describes it: *bien dans sa peau* (to be comfortable in your skin). Many French women I've observed seem to have this sense of confident self-possession. This is not to say that all French women are this way. But many of them have an air that suggests they walk a confident, feminine path.

Edith Wharton wrote, "The French woman rules French life, and she rules it under a triple crown, as a business woman, as a mother, and above all, as an artist." She is the artist of her life, which she creates with aplomb.

Maybe the *panache* arises from her important cultural history. Or her deep sense of fashion. Maybe it's her well-honed pleasure sense. Or just her basic physical attributes. As Debra Ollivier says in *Entre Nous*, "[French women have] an exasperating tendency to be thin." The reality is that despite being on the slender side, the French woman comes in all sizes just like the women of any other country. Yet she has a certain something that makes her unique.

Ollivier says that the French woman is simply "self-possessed." She has a personal freedom that's perhaps a bit different from the hard-won rights many American women now exercise in business and political life. French women seem satisfied with their place as smart, opinionated female humans with sexual appetites and well-developed desires, which they may use in the workplace or political arena, as well as in personal life.

In the U.S., women who embrace their intelligence and their sexuality are sometimes ridiculed; they're "cougared" if they're deemed sexy but over 40—especially if they date younger men. The French woman on the other hand doesn't seem to care about this notion. She refuses to sacrifice her work, her family, or her personal life (or sexuality) for public approval.

The French woman's history *is* about revolution after all. Her historical sisters loved the opulence of Versailles, but they chopped the heads off rulers who tried to squash their freedoms. Today's French woman seems to have an inherited independent streak that drives her still. She doesn't suppress her brains or her sexuality in the workplace so she can advance; she capitalizes on her unique gifts and gets ahead as a female with different "assets" than a man. And French men seem to enjoy this dynamic as well.

Sometimes there's sex in the workplace for the French female. Sometimes there isn't. But sex is an accepted part of French life and work—not a debilitating career torpedo for a woman if her colleagues find out about a romance, as is sometimes the case with an American woman. This is not to say that there isn't some grumbling about discrimination in the French workplace. And the landscape is changing as the gender gap thins in France and women want the glass ceiling to disappear entirely.

But I do think the French woman is pretty clear about who she is and what she wants. Where my generation of American women reared in the 70s and 80s felt compelled to hone their intelligence and practical skills, many of us felt we had to sacrifice our sexual allure to be taken seriously. Post 2010, today's young American woman dresses and acts more as she pleases (and at my local bank, cleavage is fully on display). But it's been a long time coming to our American culture. Many of us "seasoned" American women frankly shelved our sexuality in the workplace (and sometimes in our lives). We dressed for success and perhaps lost some of the fun of being female along the way.

I frankly admire many of these unapologetic French women. Christine Lagarde is a prime example. She's the first woman president of the International Monetary Fund (IMF). Lagarde's a French woman in full who is confident, attractive, well educated, and desirable. A noted lawyer, Lagarde served in several high-ranking government positions as well as finance minister of the G8 economy before she became head of the IMF after Dominique Strauss-Kahn resigned. As a teenager, Ms. Lagarde was a medal-winning member of the French national synchronized swimming team. After receiving her baccalaureate in 1973, she went on an American Field Service scholarship to Bethesda, Maryland. There she interned at the U.S. Capitol, returning to Paris to obtain a law degree and a master's degree in English. Twice divorced and the mother of two grown sons, her current partner is Xavier Giocanti who probably has trouble keeping up with her! She's a vegetarian, rarely drinks alcohol, and cycles and swims regularly. She was named the 8th most powerful woman in the world by *Forbes* magazine in 2011. At 5'10" she's slim and tall and wears beautifully tailored Chanel suits and Hermès scarves along with fashionable jewelry and fur-lined ponchos (reportedly to soften her look).

Molly Guinness of *The Observer* quoted Andrew Hussey, a professor at the University of London Institute in Paris, who says, "[Lagarde's] unusual among French female politicians in that there's nothing coquettish about her...a lot of others—such as Segolene Royal—play on a kind of French feminine elegance." Lagarde is highly respected among men and women and is described as *"une elle a de la classe"* (a woman with class). "She has an American informality, which she combines with a sense of distance," says Dominique Moisi, a founder of the French Institute for International Relations. "She knows how important she is, but she's quite warm in spite of everything. She can be funny when she knows she needs to be funny," says Moisi.

To me, Lagarde is an example of the modern, attractive French woman maximizing her potential without compromising herself.

While our equally powerful American politician Hillary Clinton is respected but made fun of for her pant suits (and her husband's occasional antics), Lagarde seems to be regarded as simply a powerful, charming person who also happens to be a woman.

Edith Wharton, *bon vivant* and author, said that the French woman is "in nearly all respects, as different as possible from the average American woman. The French woman is grown up. Compared with the women of France the average American woman is still in kindergarten."

I'm not sure I totally agree, but there's perhaps a kernel of truth in Wharton's opinion. Certainly the French woman is unselfconscious about romance and sexuality in her life. She's skilled at discourse. She's intellectual, appreciates culture, and reveres the art of living well. She likes attractive people—at least people who strive to maximize their assets. She likes to look attractive. And she likes sex.

French women have a non-apologetic way about them. They partake of the adult things in life. They're forthright—and sometimes are criticized for being so straightforward. Colloquially, they find the Anglo-Saxon sense of modesty to be pedestrian and a bit boring.

This directness also trickles down to their children. Reportedly, French children grow up with anatomically correct dolls—male and female—so there's far less mystery about the human body. In contrast, our American children are self-conscious about their bodies and those of the opposite sex. Their play reflects some of this confusion. (Even my therapeutic human dolls are barely distinguishable as male or female. And, in general, I find my therapeutic families woefully ignorant about sexual matters and sometimes the human anatomy in general. Yes, I sometimes even have to do some coaching about "how things work" with a few of the newlywed couples I counsel.)

How did French women gain this sophistication?

For starters, there have been many powerful—and stunning—women in France's history who've set a standard for French femininity that's both smart *and* captivating. A voluptuous, political woman is even the country's official symbol! Marianne, France's national emblem, is the personification of France. She began as a spear-carrying maiden leading the charge of the French Revolution. Now she appears as a beautifully sculpted woman more geared toward the art of love than the art of war.

Marianne's likeness appears on postage stamps and coins, as well as in the form of shapely busts in town halls and law courts throughout France. In 1969, France decided to model her on real French women, starting with the incomparable Brigitte Bardot. Later, Mireille Mathieu, Catherine Deneuve, Inès de la Fressange, and Sophie Marceau lent their images. In 2000, model Laetitia Casta won the honor. Her "bust" was particularly mesmerizing. Casta was quoted as saying, "I tell people my breasts were made in Normandy from butter and *crème fraiche.*"

The French woman can never be accused of lacking confidence.

Joan of Arc (1412-1431), another legendary French woman, led an army as a humble peasant girl from the Loire Valley. Debra Ollivier calls her the first "guerrilla girl." Sadly, she was burned at the stake for her efforts. But today she's celebrated everywhere as an intrepid visionary whose feats and courage have outshined many of the royals and military men who came before and after her. (Lest we think she was all chainmail and boots, she reportedly asked the village women along her military march to give her bolts of cloth so she could turn them into dresses. Some semblance of fashion was a priority even then.)

In the 1960s of course, the French bombshell Brigitte Bardot exploded onto the world scene in the landmark film *And God Created Woman*. She epitomized the liberated woman-child. Bardot entered the French psyche with an assertive sexuality and supercharged beauty that set the French standard. She also lived her life the way she wanted it: she had affairs, married four times, and openly said she didn't enjoy being a mother. Even Simone de Beauvoir, paramour of Jean-Paul Sartre and an uber-liberated French liberal, was captivated by Bardot. Beauvoir mused, "A saint would sell his soul to the devil for nothing more than to see her dance."

Today, the typical French woman may not be leading an army to Orléans or dominating the tabloids as an international sex symbol, but she certainly marches to the front with her French vivacity. Debra Ollivier writes: "The French girl is brought up to be polite, but she is not necessarily brought up to be a good girl. Lucky her—that Anglo-Saxon imperative to be liked (and be like everyone else) is not high on her list...She is able to discriminate without ambivalence—whether it's about a skirt or a man that simply isn't right for her life."

French females just seem to have a sort of *je ne sais quoi* that's fascinating to observe, but hard to emulate. French author Catherine Texier (*Chloé l'Atlantique*) offers a perspective:

"When I was growing up in the suburbs of Paris in the 60s and trying to figure out who I wanted to be, the essence of what it was to be a French woman seemed both obvious and elusive. It was not something you could buy via the right pair of shoes or pants or haircut—although those things definitely helped. It had to do with sexual self-confidence, and a deep conviction that being a woman was different in every way from being a man. You recognized it immediately in some women—and not just in Paris and on the pages of Marie Claire and Elle, but even in tiny, obscure French provincial towns...The essence of French femininity for me: brainy, erotic, self-confident and vulnerable, yet eminently in control."

In the land that also produced such luminaries as erotic writer Anaïs Nin and icon of cool Anouk Aimée, these French women have a genealogy of "woman personified." Perhaps the French woman is the original "It" girl. The "it" being that indescribable something that keeps one looking at her—and wanting her. Certainly Diane de Poitiers was one of the original French "It" girls.

Diane de Poitiers (1499-1566) was King Henri II's mistress despite her being 20 years older. In her youth, de Poitiers initiated the young prince into the fine art of love. Later, he couldn't bear to give her up—despite finally marrying the Italian, Catherine de Medici. Catherine de Medici was another formidable, albeit homely woman, who came to dominate France. But she lacked de Poitiers's considerable talents, especially in the boudoir.

De Poitiers was disciplined, political, and dazzling. Her portraits highlight her creamy skin, ripe breasts, and kissable neck. She allegedly started each day with a cold bath at 6 a.m. Then she climbed on a horse for a three-hour ride to maintain her youthful figure. She kept to a strict diet, often swam in the Cher River (which she reportedly entered through a trap door in the floor of her boudoir), had regular massages, treated herself to various beauty treatments and perfumed oil wraps, and drank gold bouillon as a form of beauty elixir. She was loved by the court, lavished with jewels and gifts, and reportedly never lost her sexual prowess.

Along the way, she burnished the ageless French beauty persona. She lived much of her life at the magnificent Chenonceau castle (a gift from the king). She was the only royal French mistress to have a coin minted in her likeness. And she wielded more power than Queen Catherine de Medici until the king unfortunately expired in 1559 from a lance through his brain during a jousting match. The Queen exacted her revenge of course, taking over Chenonceau and kicking de Poitiers out on her lovely *derrière*. She retired to a smallish castle outside Paris until she died at the age of 67. Interestingly, de Poitiers's body was exhumed at one point. A mega amount of gold was found in her remains. The doctors of the day pronounced that metal poisoning had hastened her demise.

Artistically, the French female is a source of infinite fascination for France. I saw one of the most interesting examples of this in the Rodin museum one summer. Auguste Rodin was apparently fascinated by the female form. In his sculpture called *Iris, Messenger of the Gods,* he took great pains to depict in detail that special part of the female anatomy (shown in this photo).

Certainly we have pornography in America (as in most countries). I would suggest this Rodin masterpiece isn't exactly pornographic sculpture, but that it's instead a work of French classical art. Readers may differ. It was particularly interesting to me as a therapist to ponder how much time Rodin must have spent painstakingly sculpting this female subject's most intimate areas. (At the risk of being crass or sounding too American, I hesitate to think of the poor woman who had to pose for this enthralling piece of statuary.) But I think the piece speaks to the French female's womanliness—and the French man's unabashed appreciation of it. The French woman understands—and uses—her womanly features.

Inès de la Fressange, model, author, and fashion icon should know: "You'll never hear a Parisian complain that her skirt is too short, her dress too tight, or her heels too high. Fashionistas and style gurus all come to the same conclusion. 'The secret of great style is to feel good in what you wear.' The Parisian knows her shape, what suits her, and what matches her lifestyle. If you don't feel comfortable in a plunging sweater, skin-tight jeans, and killer heels, go home and change."

The French woman's simply "got it"—and she's not afraid to flaunt it. That's part of what Mireille Guiliano is talking about in her book *French Women Don't Get Fat*. Stylish French women don't *allow* themselves to get fat. They value themselves too much! Despite the rich diet of wine, butter, cheese, meat, cream, and *baguettes*, just 10-15% of French adults are overweight or obese compared with America's colossal 64% (and climbing). The French woman is enviably in control of herself and her appetites—although she seems to really enjoy the pleasures she *does* allow herself.

Like many women, the French woman also judges herself. Probably few of them would ever tell you they have self-doubts, although fellow author and French woman Corine Gantz is not afraid to reveal her shortcomings. Her delightful book *Hidden in Paris* is a charming novel about three women in France (all Americans) who face failures but blossom in Paris. Interestingly, Gantz now lives in Los Angeles and in a very *un*Frenchlike way (to my mind) she's not afraid to admit, with a smile, that she weighs more than she'd like.

On the streets of Paris, however, the French woman may *appear* aloof and unaware—but she is *looking* nevertheless, sizing up the competition. I've felt this French scrutiny when I've been traipsing around Paris dressed in jeans and loafers. The "Size Up" usually begins at my face, then swiftly drops down to my sensible shoes.

Soon it drifts beyond me in a flash of dismissive boredom. I've been relegated to the "just a tourist" category.

Once, however, I keenly felt the fashion-conscious Parisian's steely assessment. My spouse and I were strolling past the Hotel Ritz one night on a walk to an important dinner. I was swathed in a sleek new trench coat that I'd purchased on Boulevard Haussmann. My hair was carefully coifed. My makeup was sultry. I'd applied rich, red lipstick, donned textured stockings, slithered into a short, black skirt, and stepped into spiky heels. I'd added a fur collar sweater that peeked out of my trench and pulled on my black leather gloves. I'd also dabbed expensive perfume behind my ears. Off I went, walking with my handsomely-dressed husband.

Two French women about 35 came around the corner and walked toward us. Suddenly, I got the "Size Up." It was like being caught in a laser beam; I could literally feel the heat. I imagined I saw the pupils of these women's eyes dilate like the eyeballs of a pair of sharks honing in on competition for dinner.

The eyes ignored my face at first. They went straight to my fur collar. Then they slid down the black trench, took in the short, black skirt and the textured stockings winding down my legs. The eyes then dropped to my slinky black heels. Then they glanced back up at my earrings, panned to my evening bag, and finally scrutinized my face. When I presumed they recognized that I was older than them by a couple of decades, the "Size Up" faded. They passed by us and never missed a beat in their conversation.

But the scrutiny hit me like a ton of bricks.

I'd had the French "once over." Translation: *"Who are you? That's a very French outfit. How do you measure up? What are your flaws?"*

I nearly burst out laughing as the realization hit me. (My husband didn't notice any of it, of course.) Was I competition? I doubt it. But the French woman has a discriminating eye, which she uses on herself as well as others. She's keen to be at her best at all times.

But does the French girl's zeal for beauty demand too high a price? I was pondering this conundrum of beauty at a price when I came upon a photo shoot along the Seine River one morning and decided to snap a picture. The crew was preparing a pretty, young French girl for a magazine spread. I noticed that not only was the model lean and lovely—all of the photographic staff was as well!

I certainly admire the French woman's skill with physical maintenance and appetite control. But do they overdo it? Some of them make me worry, frankly. When I see a waif-thin French woman on the streets of Paris, I've considered whether I should ask them if they'd like me to buy them a *baguette*. (I once saw an alarmingly anorexic woman on a corner in Cannes. Her limbs were sticking out of her adorable sundress like arms on a scarecrow, and she swayed dangerously when a gust of wind whipped past her. To me, she looked more like a concentration camp survivor than a Fashionista.)

Are French women anorexic? And are a growing number of them on a trajectory for an early exit? Most estimates suggest that 75% of women in the Western world are size 10 or greater. Paris was slow to come around to the idea that the French fashion industry might want to accommodate this shopping group. Even a decade ago, it was hard to find shops with European sizes greater than 36 or 38 (American sizes 8 and 10). Happily, plus sizes or *grandes tailles* can now be found in most of the larger stores (Bon Marche's

Encore department, Galeries Lafayette's full figure department, and Printemps). Some of the smaller shops also feature the larger size lines like Alain Weiz, C&A, Gerlane, H&M, and Cazak, to name a few. And not just tourists buy there; some French women are loosening their garters, so to speak, gaining a kilo or two, and opting for less form-fitting clothes.

But trouble may indeed be brewing. Sadly, a recent French study shows that anorexia is now a serious and growing problem in France. Just over 8% of French women ages 15-25 are anorexic. In France, the proportion of thin women has long been the highest in Europe. Around 6.7% of all French women are considered dangerously thin. French females on average score low on the Body Mass Index (BMI), the measure of weight that takes into account someone's height. They have the lowest BMIs in Europe: 23.2 on average. British women have the highest with 26.2, a level regarded as overweight. Italians have the second lowest BMIs, followed by Austrians, Germans, and Danes. The American female BMI average is a whopping 28.1!

Britons and Americans are also larger all around than the French. According to a study released in 2004 by the National Center for Health Statistics, the average height of an American woman is 5 feet 4 inches and the average weight is 164.3 pounds. The average French woman is just over 5 feet 3 inches tall and weighs 137.6 pounds (compared to 5 feet 2 ½ inches tall and 133.6 pounds in 1970). And the French eat less, despite all that bread and cheese. The average calorie consumption in the United States is about 3,642 per day against 3,551 in France. It's a small difference, but one that can add up to a five-pound weight gain in just six months.

French women have a lot of pressure to stay beautiful. And the vast French pharmaceutical and beauty industry has stepped up to "help." A *New York Times* article by Ann Morrison explored the lengths the French woman goes to for beauty:

> "If Frenchwomen don't walk enough to stay *'en forme'* there is always a pill, a lotion, a machine or a treatment to do the trick. Pharmacies have counters full of diet and figure-improving remedies. One cream promises, 'accelerated reduction in the areas resistant to diet' (hips, thighs and buttocks). Capsules assure a flatter stomach in four weeks...Frenchwomen also recommend facials, massages and spa 'cures' in their campaign against wrinkles, cellulite and saggy bottoms, bellies and breasts. One spa favorite is thalassotherapy, the seawater-based treatment that originated in France. It involves water jets, seaweed wraps, mud baths and sea-fog inhalation, meant to improve circulation, promote sleep, tone muscles and reduce cellulite. Some women are resourceful enough—or have legitimate medical reasons, like arthritis—to get doctors' prescriptions for weeks at their favorite spa. That means government health insurance covers much of the bill."

So even the French government wants to pay to keep their women beautiful!

Anorexia of course is not the answer to life-long beauty in my opinion, even in France. I hope France begins to treat the problem (and by all accounts the government, among other entities, have been alerted). But the French women who *do* take a balanced approach to health and life-long beauty are still an inspiration.

So what can we Americans learn from the French woman? Debra Ollivier suggests: "The French girl understands that sexy is a state of mind. Her relationship to food and body is sensual, not tyrannical [in general], and she takes pleasure in both. (This may explain why the French are often preoccupied with food and sex, and Anglo-Saxons with work and money.)"

The French woman shows her attractiveness not only by how she looks, but also by what she says and how she uses her brain. French girls don't typically flaunt their sexuality the way some American women do. For example, the French girl may dress to show off her sexy legs or her sexy *décolletage* (chest), but she won't do both in the same outfit. In America, some of our females show bare breasts, bare legs, and curvy behinds all in the same outfit. The French would consider this crude rather than sexy. American women who flaunt themselves in Europe, in general, are perceived as aggressively sexual.

My friend Jean-Pierre says the difference between French women and American women is that "French women are more comfortable with their bodies. And they're okay with being naked, wandering around the house. They wear clothes beautifully of course, but when it comes time to take them off, they don't hesitate. They don't care about their flaws. American women are terrified of being seen, and judged poorly. Americans can't see how their flaws are their unique features. Only that they are devastating—and must be hidden."

Does this make the legendary French woman a *coquette*? I don't know. What makes a coquette exactly? Allure mixed with restraint? Sex underpinned by intelligence? Of course, I'm generalizing here, but the French female seems to me to be emotionally and sexually assertive without having to be aggressive in a negative way. She asks for what she wants, and she gets it or moves on. She seems to embrace her sexuality as a platform for experiencing her own sexual pleasures, rather than as bait for securing a relationship. She seems to be independent, not co-dependent. My sense is that fewer French women hang on to "losers" as mates because they have more freedom to choose other partners. Some American women could benefit from embracing that idea.

On the negative side, does this mean French women are cold, unapproachable, and chronically competitive? I've read that French women don't have close girlfriends, especially because there's a certain fear that their pretty girlfriend might become their husband's next lover.

My personal experience has been that I've found many French women approachable and willing to relate—if they're approached respectfully. I once stayed at a lovely *chambre d'hôtes* (bed and breakfast) in the countryside run by a wonderful French couple, Claude and Cécile. Next to his delightful swimming pool, Claude had a large vegetable garden he was devoted to since his retirement from a high tech software company. Cécile was the manager and chef. She would prepare our sumptuous breakfast each day then serve it on Relais & Châteaux china. She often dressed in pistachio-hued silk slacks, wore elegant jewelry, and click-clacked around in darling kitten heels. She'd emerge from the kitchen with a three-tiered platter of pastries and a French press of bubbling coffee looking like she'd just stepped out of a French film.

Cécile was friendly and approachable. I was very frustrated that I couldn't speak to her more, because at the time my French was almost non-existent. She also communicated that she wished she could talk to me more, although she admitted she spoke very little English. Once her English-speaking daughter arrived, we talked nonstop with the daughter as translator. Despite the stories of standoffish French women, I found both Cécile and her daughter to be warm and welcoming. Though they were both fashionable and they appreciated some of the things I was traveling with (like hair ornaments), I felt a friendly curiosity between us. We were in sync.

When we were about to depart, Cécile's daughter told me, "We don't hug in France. We kiss (cheeks). But I have never hugged an American before, and I would like to try with you." We hugged, and she held on to me for almost a full minute. It brought tears to my eyes, because she seemed so genuine and well meaning. I felt simpatico with her. It remains a cherished memory.

The French woman certainly has a mystique. Sometimes she shares herself in disarming ways. Sometimes she exhibits herself in ways that shock and amaze. My acquaintance Danielle comes to mind in this regard.

Danielle and her husband run a small inn in France. Danielle also paints—particularly the female form. In her sultry red sitting room just off the living room of her antique-filled inn, her art is on display. Not surprisingly, Danielle's paintings feature people in dramatic poses, often in the nude, sometimes coupling. She also paints female nudes in arresting positions as shown in this photo. As a therapist, I would say her art is beautifully projective. That is, she's projecting herself, her life, and her dreams into her art. Danielle is just another example of those daring French women in full, not afraid to express—and live—their own brand of French *joie de vivre*.

In sum, the French woman is sexy, smart, and unwilling to bury her gifts. By age 12, she probably already exhibits some of this extraordinary confidence bequeathed by her feminine legacy (just watch the movie *Gigi*). With age, I suspect the charm of a French woman only increases with the years. And in the words of my friend

Jean-Pierre, "The only thing more alluring than a young, attractive French woman is a mature, attractive French woman with plenty of experience—and stories to tell."

Virility

"Présente je vous fuis; absente, je vous trouve; dans le fond des forêts votre image me suit." ("Present I flee; absent, I find you; in the depths of the forest your image follows me.")
—Jean Racine, *Phèdre*

Only a French man could get away with this kind of florid language. (Well, all right, perhaps a few poets could.) But the French male's reputation as a seducer of thought, body, and soul is legendary.

Some people find the men of France charming, self-possessed, and flirtatious. Others find them picky and a bit effete. In Paris, you can certainly see them on the street with their colorful scarves knotted below their chins, their tight pants and leathery jackets buffering them against the chill, and often with a cigarette hanging out of their mouths. Of course, there are also some overweight, out of shape *hommes Français* with plumber's cracks and *merde*-flavored language.

I've run into both.

In general, however, that French virility works wonders. French men know they are heirs to a legendary French charisma that can open doors for them all of their lives—if they use it right. By all accounts, they begin learning it at their mothers' knees. Then they cultivate it in the businesses and boudoirs of France.

Above all, the men of France are audacious. A classic example is Bernard Kouchner. Kouchner is the French cofounder of Doctors Without Borders; he later became one of France's top politicians. Handsome, erudite, and captivating, he's sometimes deemed pushy and entitled. He has even been accused of staging media opportunities for himself.

When it came time to discuss an important political appointment in 2009 with Madeleine Albright, then U.S. Secretary of State, Albright was already predisposed to dislike Kouchner. Knowing this, he revved into a full charm offensive. The wily Kouchner found out that Albright had been born in the mountains of central Europe. So he scooped up a bunch of edelweiss flowers and presented them to her when they met, reminding her of her beautiful childhood. Of course he did a lot of persuasive talking too (in French-accented English). By the end of the meeting, Albright confessed in her book *Madam Secretary* that she found him "irresistible." Classic French charm—and a few country flowers—had won the day.

For French men in general, this *séduction* skill can be platonic, political, sexual, or cultural. Some call it "soft power." The modern Paris male on the street may not be Napoléon Bonaparte, but he has a heritage of a suave power that's potent. Actor Jean Dujardin is a wonderful example of a French male wielding his powers of seduction. Dujardin was the star of the much-lauded "silent" film *The Artist*. He won the American best actor Academy Award Oscar in 2012—the first French man ever to do so. His poignant, funny performance as the has-been silent screen star wowed audiences. And the fact that he only spoke a smattering of English made him even more endearing to the public. When he and Meryl Streep posed for pictures, she beamed like a schoolgirl as Dujardin laid his head on her shoulder. She looked enchanted.

Truly, who could resist?

Dujardin follows in the footsteps of performers like Yves Montand and Maurice Chevalier who parlayed their French charm into cinematic stardom. Dujardin injects his own quirky brand of French pizzazz into everything he does. And by all accounts, he's another French performer well on his way to lifelong adoration.

Dujardin originally began his career as a stand-up comedian. Later, he portrayed the original James Bond in the OSS 117 spy films made in France. (OSS was the precursor to the modern-day CIA during World War II.) I stumbled onto Dujardin as the superspy long before he made *The Artist*. Flipping on TV5 Monde (French television) one morning, the camera panned a room of mini-skirted dancers cavorting with a toothy, dark-haired man in clingy ski clothes playing with a magic balloon. A cadre of evil thugs suddenly crashed through the door. The man pulled out a revolver and blasted them all. The main lovely thanked him with a sultry kiss. Soon they were off to her boudoir with a pair of brandies, while turtledoves cooed in the background. It all felt vaguely familiar.

Since the dialogue was all in French (no subtitles), I was a bit fuzzy about what was going on. But I couldn't take my eyes off the "hero" played by none other than Jean Dujardin. (Later I found a subtitled version, and my husband and I watched the film again. It was even better with English subtitles! As is typical with the French male's power of seduction, my husband was equally as smitten with Dujardin as I was—in a platonic sort of way.)

I soon discovered that Dujardin was actually playing OSS 117, the original secret spy character dreamed up by Jean Bruce. In 1949, Bruce first wrote about the handsome French agent called OSS 117, code name for Hubert Bonisseur de La Bath. De la Bath is a former OSS officer who works undercover with agencies like the CIA and MI-6. He spies, he shoots, he loves—not necessarily in that order.

It turns out that Bruce's work *predates* Ian Fleming's James Bond books by four years. I suspect Fleming "borrowed" the idea for an undercover spy who is catnip to the ladies from novelist Bruce. In England, "OSS 117" became "007" and "Hubert Bonisseur de la Bath" became "James Bond."

Bruce went on to write 91 OSS 117 novels for the French publishing house *Fleuve Noir Espionnage.* In 1963, following Jean Bruce's death in a car crash while driving his Jaguar (how French is that?), his wife took up the franchise. Josette Bruce produced *another* 143 titles under her own name. After *her* death, the series continued with her daughter and stepson who together wrote another 24 titles! As today's OSS 117, Dujardin (pictured)

seems to personify everything the classic French man is supposed to be: a witty, crafty, and suave lover of women.

French men are reared to enjoy women. And they expect the admiration to be reciprocated. I've certainly felt the "heat." My friendly French concierge, "Jacques," is an example. Jacques (pictured) called to me one March morning across the lobby of my hotel in the 16th arrondissement. Jacques spoke perfect English, of course. Over several days, we became friends, particularly because every time I came through the lobby, he'd beckon me over to the concierge desk with yet another tray of warm *Gougères* (French cheese puffs) straight from the oven. I'd reach for a treat, then another and another. He seemed delighted to watch me stuff my mouth with *Gougères* while we conversed about the day's events.

Jacques told me he had worked for the same hotel chain in New York as well as other international locations. Now back in Paris, he apparently retained some of the candor he'd learned in America. When he found out I was an American therapist specializing in couples treatment, Jacques volunteered that he was on his third marriage. He rolled his eyes and quipped, "That's why I have to work so hard—too many wives to support."

"By the way," he went on, checking his reservation data, "When is *your* husband arriving? I believe it's tomorrow."

"Yes," I answered, "tomorrow around 2 pm."

"Ah," he responded. "And so what are you going to do today before he arrives, Madame?"

"I'm going to Printemps (department store)."

"Hmmm," he grinned and gave me *le regarde* (that penetrating French flirtation look). "Well, since he is not here yet, I will be your husband and tell you: Don't spend too much money!"

I burst out laughing.

I was charmed of course; I didn't feel the least harassed. In America, no concierge would be so forward as to "pose" as my husband. But in Paris, *c'est la façon dont le Français* (it's the way of the French man).

In *French Toast*, Harriet Welty Rochefort suggests that in general, "many French men have a wonderful sense of humor and a love of the whole flirting game. [But] France is probably the one country an attractive single woman can [still] live peacefully, because a woman is allowed to take or leave the attentions men lavish on her. To be more explicit: If you tell a man to bug off, he will."

But a French man is also not afraid of the serious side of flirtation. And he's not afraid to touch. French men *bise* (kiss) cheeks regularly (even with each other). The hand kiss (*baisemain*) is also a legendary French technique. And there are several styles of *baisemain* for those who wonder. Hovering above the hand, for instance, so that the kissee can feel the subtle breath of the kisser but not make skin contact translates to a friendly, non-sexual *baisemain*. When the kisser presses his lips into the woman's hand lightly, however, it becomes a heightened *baisemain* and translates to a familiar (or "I would like it to be more familiar") relationship. But when the lips linger on the hand, moving up and down in a foreplay manner, it becomes an *effleurer*. Fireworks are about to erupt. Translation: "*Voulez vous coucher avec moi ce soir*"? ("Will you sleep with me tonight?") I feel certain most French men are adept at all styles.

The French man has a renaissance heritage, after all. He's reared around first-class fashion, fine wine, good food, lively discourse, acclaimed artistry, exquisite poetry, and legendary romance lore. He often has an inherent sense of style. Unlike many American men, he's comfortable discussing style, fabrics, silhouettes, colors, and accessories. He knows how to bring flowers, candy, and jewelry to important people in his life. He's often skilled at writing and pens his feelings as well as speaks about them.

The virile French male is often skilled as *le seducer* in the bedroom. By many reports, he's trained to take time with foreplay (verbal or otherwise). He learns to linger over the act of sex, taking time and seeking a high-quality experience. This is not to say that every French man is a sophisticated lover. But the stereotype probably exists for a reason. The men of France say they're inclined to explore a woman's body like a mystery, seeking the special places that stimulate her. American men are colloquially more likely to focus solely on the common core erogenous zones—and as a clinician treating marital issues, I hear a great deal about this problem. I can't speak to the gay French experience. But I suspect that many French lovers are equally as adept here as well.

L'homme Français is also an intellectual seducer. France's history is based on revolutionary ideas that culminated in acts of liberation, equality, and fraternity. Even the Four Musketeers tore their way across the country fighting and loving with the motto: *One for All and All for One.*

In the movie *Funny Face*, Audrey Hepburn is mesmerized by a French intellectual called Professor Emile Flostre. The handsome professor is busy using his intellectual prowess on Hepburn's naïve American character. Suddenly, Fred Astaire (as Dick Avery) bursts through the door and "rescues" her from the French cad. The American gets the girl, of course (since it's an American film). But quite a few female fans have told me they still had their eyes on the professor.

Smart *and* sexy? It's a powerful combination.

The intellectual in France is revered as a seducer *avec* ideas. He enchants men, women, children—everyone—with his concepts. It was French man René Descartes, after all, who wrote: *Je pense, donc je suis* (I think, therefore I am). France's history is steeped in big-brained French men who shaped France as a country and a culture. Descartes championed philosophy and math. Voltaire, Rousseau, and Diderot brought down a monarchy and designed a new democracy. Sartre and Camus evolved the French existential philosophy that underpins much of French life today.

Men in France are reared to be persuasive, but to be persuasive with their ideas as well as their bodies. "It is not enough to conquer, one must also know how to seduce," Voltaire wrote. And even a few American men have spent time in France, learning the powers of intellectual and cultural seduction.

Thomas Jefferson, America's third President, wrote glowingly of his time in Paris. He lived there for five years from 1784-1789 as the American representative of Congress. Apparently, there was quite a bit of cultural swapping between Jefferson and his peers. He even helped craft the ideas in the 1789 *Declaration of the Rights of Man*, a foundational document for the French Revolution.

Jefferson (as well as Benjamin Franklin) cherished the French lifestyle. And he was embraced by the French for his intellectualism, his manners, and his stately bearing. Jefferson waxed eloquent about walking the byways of the Tuileries. He visited the Palais Royal, shopped at Les Halles, and studied the Panthéon. He enjoyed seeing plays by Racine and Molière, and he examined as many bookstores as he could. He loaded up on furniture, kitchen utensils, candlesticks, teapots, fabrics, seeds, plants, and various other items. When he reluctantly returned to America, he sent back 86 packing crates! Even Jefferson went shopping in Paris. He felt so well treated there that he wrote: "Every man has two countries—his own and France." Did Jefferson pick up some French-inspired charisma while he was there? By all accounts he did since he was finally elected President of the United States in 1801—after two tries.

When it comes to women, the French male has perhaps a wider appreciation of the female form than the American male. French men are particularly appreciative of a woman's "backend curves," for example. You'll find many of these depicted in French art and photography. The "bottom" is variously referred to as the *derrière*; more commonly it's called *fesses*. *Fesses* don't refer to anything as crass as the "butt." Instead, this alludes to the whole, rounded area of a beautiful woman's nether regions.

Elaine Sciolino in *La Seduction* cites a poll by the BVA organization (a French market research firm) regarding male responses to women's bodies. The poll states *"only 38 percent of French men found the most fascination in a woman's breasts...50 percent preferred her fesses and legs."* American men, on the other hand, may be partial to breasts (hence we American women catch them when their eyes slide to our chests). But a savvy French man can stand on the corner of Rue de Rivoli  and Avenue de L'Opera and admire a woman's *fesses* from behind them completely unnoticed. Brigitte Bardot sparked the quintessential remark on this phenomenon. In the film, *And God Created Woman*, one of the male characters says when she walks by: "She has an ass that sings."

But some French men go too far. In 2011, Dominique Strauss-Kahn, then future candidate for the French presidency, was arrested for forcing a maid in a New York hotel to have oral sex with him.

He was arrested, charged, and ultimately released. He reportedly paid the victim an undisclosed sum in a civil suit.

In America he was vilified.

In France, as Elaine Sciolino points out in *La Seduction*, "Strauss-Kahn [at first became] a living legend, and some people expressed quiet admiration that such a high-profile political figure could find time for such an active social life." However, the tide soon turned against Strauss-Kahn—even in France. When sex ring allegations later surfaced, basically categorizing him as a purveyor of prostitution, he lost all credibility. Even Former Socialist Prime Minister Michel Rocard called him "sick."

The majority of French men, however, are reared to admire, love, and pursue women in healthier ways. They're taught by their mothers and grandmothers to value the female nature. And to do it with reverence. They learn to appreciate the differences between male and female perspectives—and use them in their everyday flirtations as the spice of life. He may grow up to be a flirt, but the French male is not necessarily promiscuous, as his legacy might suggest. He flirts, but it may stop there. Or it may not. Nothing is taken for granted.

The man reared in France definitely has a certain something. He can be charming, erudite, demanding, and exasperating. Many French men are also quite attached to their mothers, by all reports. French men typically go home to their mother's house once a week for dinner, at the very least. If they're married and have children, everyone goes. Family is very important for French males, and this is part of the reason many of them stay married, even if they dally elsewhere.

The French man is complex, mercurial, emotional. "I like French men very much," American chanteuse Josephine Baker who found fame in Paris once said, "because even when they insult you they do it so nicely." But perhaps Sharon Santoni on her blog, "My-FrenchCountyHome," said it best:

"The true [French man] is temperamental...He can be the most charming and irresistible person you have ever met and he can be arrogant and plain difficult. But maybe therein lies his charm...He wants to please and be pleased...Flirting and charming is second nature to him...He dresses well, likes to look dashing, loves good shoes. He can carry off that wonderful air of elegance and ease, smart without looking uncomfortable... He is happy to joke, but happier still to argue...about anything; the state of the world; the best way to cook his favorite dish, the merits of the latest film...He loves his children, he doesn't feel ridiculous buying flowers, he wears perfume, he enjoys the opera and good restaurants, he knows about wine. He can talk about books, politics, women, food and sport. He is an accomplisher."

Indeed, he is French. What more can be said?

Passion

"Je serai poète et toi poésie." ("I'll be a poet, and you'll be poetry.") — François Coppée

The French take great delight in demonstrating their considerable skill in lovemaking. Passion and romance are inextricably linked in the French concept of *amour*. Sex without romance would be considered gauche in France. Through films like *L'Histoire d'Adèle H*, *Gigi*, *Le Divorce*, and *A Man and a Woman*, we get a cinematized look at the intricacies of French passion. But it's quite another thing to see it up close and personal.

I entered the trendy bar at the Park Hyatt Paris-Vendôme one Friday night. The dark paneled bar was sleek, with white columns and plush carpets. Lounge music played subtly in the background. The intimate tables were lit with perfumed candles. The drinks were pricey. Most of the clientele was dressed for Friday night cocktails and perhaps an expensive Parisian dinner somewhere.

My husband and I were seated in an alcove of four tables. The couple on our left was speaking in quiet French. The young woman sat on the bench seat to my immediate left; she was probably in her late 20s. She had cropped, elegantly arranged red hair, creamy skin (from what I could see in the dim light), and bejeweled earrings. She was dressed in a black sheath and wore dark high-heeled pumps. The man, also in his late 20s or early 30s, was seated across from her. He was dressed in a dark suit and tie, with a camel-colored scarf slung casually around his shoulders. Neither wore wedding rings.

It seemed to me that they were having a very serious discussion in French, perhaps of a business or political nature. They were not "cooing" at each other as if on a date; they appeared cerebral and almost argumentative. I wasn't eavesdropping exactly, but our close proximity created a little bubble of intimacy for all of us and allowed me to overhear the conversation.

During the next half hour, our very formal waiter offered menus, delivered drinks, picked up dishes, and kept a watchful eye on our little area. I always enjoy connecting with people, so he and I shared some pleasantries as my husband and I sipped our drinks. The four of us continued chatting and noshing quietly with what I would describe as "studied restraint."

Suddenly, I noticed our waiter move in from the right toward the other couple's table. He had their bill in his hand. He then abruptly stopped, motionless. At the same time, I sensed a dramatic movement to my left. I turned ever so slightly to witness the business couple suddenly stand up and lunge at each other over their tiny cocktail table. Their lips pressed together in a passionate, lengthy kiss. It lasted so long that I turned back to the waiter who was now looking back and forth between the lip-locked couple and me. He was trying not to laugh, but the more he and I looked at each other as the couple kept on kissing, the more difficult it was to keep a straight face. Pretty soon, the waiter and I were giggling.

At long last, the couple parted and sat back. The server sprang forward and presented them with their bill. In seconds, the man had paid and the pair sprang up like jack rabbits—probably heading to some Parisian pied-à-terre for a quick tryst.

Voilà! Love French style.

From that moment on, the server treated me differently. He knew my husband and I were Americans, of course. I also sensed he knew that he and I had shared one of those humorous, cultural collision moments that needs no explanation. *Une liaison amoureuse* had taken precedence over *le tâche* (task), and it was fun to watch the waiter "just deal with it."

My take away: the French don't mess around when it comes to love. They're forthright about what they want and when they want it. Romance and flirting is expected in France; it acts as a glue to many relationships, providing a titillating subtext to interactions personal or professional. The French have centuries of courtship customs, of course. Among them is an elegant, flirting banter called *marivaudage*, named after the 18th century French playwright *Marivaux*. It's light, flirty, and above all, well, French. Sometimes it doesn't even look like flirting. In fact, my friend Barbara says, "I once listened to a French couple flirting with each other and it sounded like a sparring match!" (All the more reason I missed the seduction underway between the couple at the Park Hyatt.)

I think all this French flirting is confusing for some Americans. In America, it's pretty easy to get through a day without flirtatious banter (although a few might argue). While it can't be said that Americans never flirt (and I treat plenty of couples who are concerned that their spouse has crossed the line with others on this), it's certainly not looked upon in general in our culture as acceptable *or* even expected. We Americans are friendly, but we tend to frown on open flirtation. In America, we're more likely to hide a sexually flirtatious, non-endorsed liaison (e.g., "cheating" or "soon to be cheating") from public view. But the French think nothing of flaunting it!

In France, flirting and flattery are commonplace. They're often done with some level of sexual undertones, but intercourse is not necessarily a *fait accompli*. French men are also flattered when *others* flirt with their partners; they would be insulted if their partner was *not* considered attractive. Flirtation greases the skids, so to speak, in French business interactions as well. Even heterosexual same-sex individuals are complimentary to each other.

My sister and I once went on a Bateaux Mouche Seine River dinner cruise. We were inundated by servers showering us with comments about how beautiful and charming we were. At first, I thought we were special in getting all this attention. I later learned that almost *everyone* on the cruise got similar treatment!

It's very important to understand that not all of this French flirting leads back to the boudoir. But having regular sex is certainly embraced by most of the French. Affairs aren't necessarily frowned upon. Former mistresses and future mistresses are often found among family friends or casual associates. Sex (in marriage or out) even in the later years is actively sought.

My friend Carla even recalls sitting in a Paris *café* that was attached to a hotel. She was enjoying a late afternoon coffee with her husband at a table near the bottom of a long set of stairs leading to the upper floors of the hotel. Around 6:30 p.m. she couldn't help but notice a constant stream of couples descending from the stairs and then passing out to the street through the *café*. She finally got up the nerve to ask her server about this "traffic." He patiently explained that this was the *cinq à sept*, the time traditionally used between 5:00 and 7:00 p.m. for having "*les affaires.*" Apparently many couples pop in for an "encounter" so they can be home for dinner with their spouses by 8:00!

Sometimes the French go even further with *amour*. (And this photo of a couple in the Luxembourg Gardens suggests the pair wasn't holding back.) In her book *All You Need to be Impossibly French*, Helena Frith Powell tells the story of a French woman who said she actually used her lovers as a workout. Her idea was that since men had been using women for decades, why not use men as objects of exercise? Ap-

parently, she preferred popping home for a rendezvous rather than nipping out to the gym for her exercise and toning.

American girls in France enjoy talking about the French male's approach to love as well. My friend Kate (who attended two years of college in Paris) says, "A French guy gets your information, then calls right away. There's no playing around and waiting for days before he calls you. He gets right to it." On the other hand, Kate says French girls are very clear about whether they like a French guy or not. If the girl likes the guy, she'll flirt back. If not, she'll rudely interrupt the guy in mid-sentence and tell him to get lost. Kate explained, "Parisian girls don't look anyone in the eye unless they want to initiate contact."

The French see themselves as attractive and smart. And they like partners who embody the same qualities. There's an expression in France: *avoir du chien*. It means to be sexy, attractive, and brainy. The French aren't only attracted to a partner's outer appearance; they're also attracted to what's in the partner's brain. Many romantic French films include a healthy dose of philosophic banter that populates the French relationship. For example, in the famous François Truffaut film *Jules et Jim*, Jeanne Moreau is busy seducing two best friends, Jules and Jim. The film has a little sex, but an enormous amount of cerebral foreplay in which the meaning of life and love is discussed endlessly. It was a big hit. Sex without philosophy is frankly a bore in France.

Despite the liberal approach to sex (and public displays of it as shown), however, the French can be fickle about how passion plays itself out in life—especially if their political leaders are dabbling too much. For example, Valérie Trierweiler, the current first lady of France, has created some controversy with her lover, French President François Hollande. The comely Ms. Trierweiler is a political journalist and long-time writer for France's weekly news magazine *Paris Match*. Dubbed "The Rottweiler" by some due to the unrelenting way she pursues political stories, she displayed similar doggedness in pursuing Hollande while he was still partnered with his long-time paramour, Ségolène Royal.

Royal had been with Hollande for 30 years and borne him four children when Trierweiler caught the President's eye. Not only was Royal originally President Hollande's partner, she was a significant political force in her own right. In all their years together, the two had reached the heights of the Socialiste party. But as he began a serious run for the highest office in France, Hollande dumped Royal for the comely Trierweiler. He ultimately won the Presidency.

Interestingly, Hollande had campaigned on a platform of serious respectability as *"Monsieur Normal."* This ran in opposition to then President Nicholas Sarkozy's image as *"Monsieur Bling Bling"* whose conspicuous private life with wife and supermodel Carla Bruni was ridiculed in the French press. When Hollande beat Sarkozy, Trierweiler ill advisedly took to her Twitter account *"in a towering rage"* against Ségolène Royal who had done little to help him get elected. Royal fired back.

Hollande, the bespectacled, balding new President was suddenly caught in a firestorm of female *pique*. Headlines in *L'Express* and *Marianne* hissed "The Poison of Jealousy" and "Secrets of a Trio From Hell." Far from being seen as a strong, presidential new leader, Hollande was cast in the media as a weak-minded male caught between two powerful women. By the way, despite France's liberal attitude toward love, Hollande is the first President in history who isn't married.

The French have an interesting attitude toward privacy when it comes to love. Elaine Sciolino attempts to explain this in *La Seduction:*

> "...Because the French believe in the right to pleasure, they are highly tolerant of other people's private behavior, especially sexual behavior. They believe that private lives must not be invaded by outsiders...American style investigative journalism [about people's sex lives] is rare in France...and libel laws are [very] protective..."

In contrast, American voters tend to see extramarital sex by their elected officials as a violation of trust. Character wise, politicians in America are expected to maintain the ideals of pure intent and pure acts, focused diligently on the task of governing. In France, however, the ability to seduce is regarded by men and women as a basic competency. Demonstrations of virility are one of the reasons to elect an official—and seldom would he be impeached for his indiscretions (unlike former President Bill Clinton).

Paradoxically, the French as a whole don't seem to mind their elected officials' open marriages and sexual escapades—as long as they don't interfere with the national welfare or dignity. As Harriet Welty Rochefort says in *Joie de Vivre*, "the French love good repartee and will forgive a lot—but not a president who cannot or will not remain above the fray."

The French citizenry was particularly irked at the funeral of President François Mitterrand in 1996. While the state casket lay on view, a notable picture was taken of six individuals standing shoulder to shoulder mourning Mitterrand's remains. They were: Danielle Mitterrand (his widow), their son Jean-Christophe, Mazarine Pingeot (the grown daughter of his mistress Anne Pingeot), Anne Pingeot (the mistress), and Mitterrand's son Gilbert Mitterrand. Yes, the country of France discovered that not only had Mitterrand kept two families during his life, but his mistress's family had been supported financially by the state, with full police protection! The citizenry grumbled mightily. For the French, sex is one thing; use of public funds to maintain one's extramarital lifestyle is quite another matter.

As they say, it's complicated.

One question is often asked by Americans, however. Do the French—politician or average Jacques—really have more sex than anyone else? Elaine Sciolino in *La Seduction* reports that Durex, the best-selling condom (*le préservatif*) manufacturer in France—and in the world—regularly publishes statistics about sexual habits. One of the polls canvassed 26,000 people in 26 countries and concluded that the French only have sex about 120 times a year. That makes them the 11th most active country behind Greece at 164 and Brazil at 145, but statistically ahead of the U.S. at a paltry 85.

The French sometimes see Americans as prudish and near-sighted, while Americans see the French headlines and wonder if French sexual freedoms have frankly gone too far. Interestingly, Dr. John Gagnon, emeritus professor of sociology at the State University of New York, studied two surveys exploring French and American sexual practices and came up with some fascinating results.

Gagnon found that Americans and the French are fairly similar in the amount of sex they have. Interestingly, Americans reported even more partners over a lifetime than the French. American men reported 19 sexual partners in a lifetime on average while French men reported only 13. American women said they had six partners on average in a lifetime, while French women only reported four. Dr. Gagnon and others have interpreted this to mean that the French may have multiple relationships, but they tend to have more monogamous relationships over a longer period with the multiple partners they do have. (Think: lifetime mistress or a second family.) Americans tend toward casual or short-term affairs. (Think: casual encounters or "one night stands.")

Still, the notion of lots of sex—and the proverbial French mistress—persists. (In this photo taken in Gare Saint-Lazare, I fantasized that these two were having a passionate affair because he kissed her so long he nearly missed his train!)

From literature, film, and historical anecdote, many French men say they feel compelled to add a third to their marital bliss in the form of a mistress in order to keep things happy. As Monsieur Vidocq says in the 1940s film, *A Scandal in Paris*, "Sometimes the chains of marriage are so heavy, they must be born by three."

In Pamela Druckerman's *Washington Post* article, "French Women Don't Get Fat and Do Get Lucky" she writes:

> "Frenchwomen seem open not just to non-marital sex but also to the extramarital variety. Overall self-reported levels of infidelity are practically identical in France and the United States. But because the taboo on cheating is weaker in France, what would be guilty flings in the United States can blossom into long love affairs over here. 'When [French] people have multiple partners, they have stable partners, and not one-night stands. This is not the case in the U.S.,' says the French researcher Alain Giami, who co-authored a paper on French and American sexual habits."

There *can* be pain nevertheless in France over some of this infidelity. Many French citizens may tell you they're very liberal, but when it comes to infidelity, their partners may not always be so forgiving. Take the case of my delightful friend Sylvie. Sadly, Sylvie had an unhappy 10-year French marriage. But her divorce turned out to be an equitable parting; they even toasted with a glass of Sylvie's alimony.

How?

Sylvie had fortuitously married into a Cognac dynasty. Her husband, Philippe, was the eldest son of a very old family near Poitou-Charentes in southwest France. Their estates included a magnificent *maison* and many, many hectares of cognac vineyards. According to Sylvie, the very air one breathed in this magical place was permeated by the heavy scent of spirits evaporating from oak casks held in storage. "The Angels' Share" they called it.

Alas, Sylvie discovered that Philippe was doing some extramarital "distilling" with a woman in nearby Jarnac. Sylvie promptly filed for divorce. When it came time to settle, she was offered her choice of generous settlements. She took cognac.

Yes, bottles and bottles of the stuff. She explained to me one evening about all the different types. Loosely translated there was light, dark, very dark, special, very special, and yes, a preferred lady's cognac that was pale and tasted of brandy and fruit. I think she had enough bottles to open her own cognac store on Boulevard Haussmann. The last time I saw her, she was showing off her tummy tuck and an elegant new coat from Printemps, and plotting whether to vacation in Cannes or Monaco.

Despite the affairs and divorces, there are still plenty of couples getting married in France, although many couples decide to cohabit instead. Statistically, there about 50 marriages performed each year for every 10,000 citizens. This is the lowest in Europe. Like the U.S., the average age for marriage in France is increasing: 30 for men and 28 for women. Many couples don't bother to get married and live together instead, but French law distinguishes between couples living together unofficially (*en union libre*) and officially (*en concubinage*). Neither is recognized under French inheritance laws. About 40% of French children are born out of wedlock, and about a fifth are raised by a single parent. Mothers—married or not—are paid a generous allowance by the state.

Divorce rates run about 33%, which is lower than in the U.S. at about 50%. The reasons for divorce vary, but one of the most interesting French causes for divorce is lack of sex. In September 2011, a 51-year-old French man in Nice was ordered to pay his ex-wife a little more than $13,000 in damages for failing to have enough sex during their 21-year marriage. The man was fined under Article 215 of France's civil code that states that married couples must agree to a "shared communal life" which includes "sex."

And so it goes.

As with American relationships, some French relationships work (see the newlyweds below on Pont Alexandre) and some don't. The French have their own unique style regarding how they dally and with whom they dally. But sex is definitely in the air in France. *Vive l'amour.*

Verve

"Alessandro and I followed an exquisite pair of legs out of the [Paris] Métro today. They were clad in flowery black lace stockings and dark red pumps. Their owner wore a coat with five buttons closing the back flap, and gloves that matched her pumps precisely. We walked briskly up the steps, and I turned around to see the front of the coat, only to find that the lady in question was at least seventy. She was both dignified and *très chic*. Old age, *à la parisienne*!

—Eloisa James, *Paris in Love*

A s of this writing, the world's oldest living person was a woman who lived 44,724 days. Not surprising, she was French.

Jeanne Calment thrived for 122 years and 164 days when she finally succumbed in 1997. When asked the secret of her longevity, she had replied, "Every day, a bit of chocolate and port wine." Madame Calment, like many other women of France, lived a long life nestled in the bosom of a French society that reveres its women, no matter how many birthdays they've celebrated.

The stunning Juliette Binoche pictured above is a ripening actress, artist, and dancer who is beautiful, articulate, and admired for her verve. She never lacks for work—or attention. She's appeared in more than 40 features, and she's been the recipient of numerous international accolades. She's also a published author, political activist, and the mother of two children. French Playboy's photo spread on Binoche carried text that gushed: "The more time passes, the more her inner beauty glows." She turns 50 in 2014.

Charlotte Rampling, *La Legende* as she's known in France, is another ripening actress who works steadily and is revered for her verve. A Brit who is now a Parisian, the dark-haired lovely star is in her 60s. But as a working actress who cares a great deal about her appearance, she's decided *not* to alter her appearance with plastic surgery. She was quoted in the UK's *Daily Mail*: "Don't change your face and you can get really interesting parts—not just granny parts; you can get sexy parts, too."

When she was 55, Rampling famously appeared naked in the French film, *Under the Sand*; she introduced a whole new generation to *La Legende's* seductive gifts. Even at 60+, Rampling appears in magazines with only a bit more on than she did in 1973 when Helmut Newton photographed her naked for *Vogue*. Rampling is now a grandmother, but her sexy print and film career has never been busier. "French women have been made beautiful by the French people—they're very aware of their bodies, the way they move and speak, they're very confident of their sexuality. French society's made them like that," she says.

What's the secret to the ripening French woman's charm?

For one thing, French men are reared to value women of all ages; they want to romance them—wrinkles or no. French men find the older French woman particularly tantalizing. She's often assertive while being appreciative and forgiving. She generally has her own money. She's relationally experienced, so French men say she's less clingy. She's also generally intelligent, culturally seasoned, and seldom boring. Of course she's often sexually skilled. Reportedly, it can be a great relief for a French man to be with a woman who knows what she needs to be satisfied—and how to get it.

Pamela Druckerman wrote in the article "French Women Don't Get Fat and Do Get Lucky" in the *Washington Post* in 2008:

"Older women in Paris don't actually look any better than the ones in New York. The difference is that the French typically don't see sex as a privilege for the young and beautiful. They see it as one of life's most basic pleasures—something women or men would not give up without a fight...Through our 40s, we American women manage to arrange romps on a fairly regular basis. But the latest national statistics show that by our 50s, a third of us haven't had sex in the last year. By our 60s, nearly half have gone sexless in the previous year. Once we hit our 70s, most of us might as well hang up an "out of business" sign...But not in France. Frenchwomen simply don't suffer from the same dramatic, post-40s slide into sexual obsolescence. Just 15 percent of Frenchwomen in their 50s and 27 percent in their 60s haven't had any sex in the past year, according to a 2004 national survey by France's Regional Health Observatory. Another national survey...reports that cohabiting Frenchwomen over 50 are having more sex now than they did in the early 1990s."

Unlike America, where there tends to be an implied expiration date of some kind on a woman's sexuality, the ripening French woman like the one depicted here expects sex—and is pursued for it regularly. She also pursues it for herself.

I stumbled on a French film called *Cliente* (billed as *A French Gigolo* in America). Directed and written by Josiane Balasko, one of the two stars, it tells the tale of two French sisters looking for love after age 40. One finds love with a robust, lusty man her age (strangely a Native American from the Midwest). The other sister pays for sex with a reluctant young French gigolo, Marco, who's torn between supporting his family and caring for the fascinating older woman who loves him and pays him to love her back.

It sounds seamy perhaps, but it was clever and artfully done. The main focus was on the relationship between the two sisters and how they cope with being normal French women growing older. They talk about their needs with passion and humor. They argue about their jobs. They voice strong opinions, but they're independent and sage. Above all, they feel liberated in making their own choices. They're not afraid to go for what they want—and each gracefully accepts what she gets.

Are older American women enjoying this same freedom? Do they feel as free to honor their own needs? In "How French Women Age: The Real Secret" in the *Huffington Post*, Deborah Ollivier writes about aging American women and their sexual behaviors compared to the French. She suggests that retaining one's beauty in America may be a top priority after 40. But having ongoing sex may not. "It helps that France is a grown-up culture, not a youth culture, where 40 and 50 year olds are 'players,' too. Witness French cinema, where the love affairs of older women are a staple... What a big contrast to the junior varsity squad that dominates American cinema!"

Ollivier also notes that living well is more the objective for the older French woman than the artificiality of striving for perennial youth.

"While older French women do, indeed, generally enjoy lives of accrued sensuality, we American women are often busy whipping ourselves into shape with a vengeance...Take a look at any American magazine for women forty-plus. Celebrations of age usually come with a clarion call for emulating youth in all its age-defying Fantastic-at-Forty-Plus firmness. As we age-defy (which, let's face it, is just shorthand for age-deny)...Huffing and puffing on the treadmill of eternal personal transformation is no picnic, and French women know it...French women sense strains of joyless utilitarianism here that conspire not only against their in-bred bon vivantism, but that it smacks of a certain Puritan self-denial gone awry. They're wary of all our aging fabulousness. They also know that cougars belong in the zoo."

Are aging French women desirable because they like love and are loved? Or are they loved because they keep the flames of desire burning? The answer is probably both. I certainly see plenty of these beautifully-coiffured, mature women on the streets of Paris who still make plenty of men's hearts beat faster.

They're often immaculately dressed like this stunning lady pictured. Their scarves, bags, high heels, and outfits flatter their figures. As they pass me on the street with their little dogs in tow (or their husbands), the delicate aroma of French perfume usually lingers in the air. They don't defer to the younger women on the street; they *own* the street.

The French culture endorses handsome, vital aging—and French women know it. They're comfortable with their maturing bodies, and they readily show them in print, on screen, and by all reports, in the boudoir. Elisabeth Weissman interviewed many older French men for the book *Un Âge Nommé Désir* (*An Age Named Desire*). She says she learned "they see in maturity a form of eroticism." An older woman in France is still considered desirable; romance and adulation are expected.

This may be one of the reasons I feel comfortable in Paris. I'm no great beauty. But I feel noticed and mostly appreciated, especially if I dress well and act with confidence. French men treat me with respect, in general; I particularly notice their eyes don't always whip past me so fast when a younger women comes into view (as is often the case in America.)

Truth be told, I feel vibrant when I stroll the streets of Paris. Walking through the glorious Tuileries after dark, with the Louvre complex twinkling behind it, I feel the grandeur of Louis the XIV in the air. As I turn, my gold scarf fluttering, I see the Champs Élysée bathed in incandescent light with the Eiffel sparking off to the left across the Seine. I watch the Parisians (and tourists) strolling in their finery, and the air is thick with French magic. And perhaps this too is one of the age-defying elements of life in France. With the grandeur and elegance of the City of Light all around, how could one not feel rejuvenated?

It's frankly a pleasure to see the example of these mature French women who desire and are desired. I notice the mature Parisian women at the cosmetic counters and the pharmacies, buying creams and lotions to pamper their faces and their skin. They're curious, but skilled at finding exactly what is right for them. French women reportedly spend about $2.2 billion a year on facial skin care—as much as Spanish, German, and British women put together.

The lingerie departments are also filled with these over 40 French women. And they're not buying granny gowns. Oh no, they're purchasing the same garter belts and *bustières* as the young ones in such bright shades as azure, lemon, peacock, crimson, and, of course, black.

The mature French woman maximizes her beauty by taking very good care of it. Beauty treatments have reached an art form in France. There are creams, preparations, balms, and mists for every part of the French female anatomy, some of which become sadly neglected by American women in the U.S. (Mature American women know what I'm talking about.)

The maturing French woman has regular facials at places like *Institut de Beauté*, a beauty consortium found all over Paris where one can have a facial, a body care treatment, or a variety of other offerings. Madame also treats herself to soothing multi-day therapies, regular massages, sea treatments, and cleanses.

Iconic designer Coco Chanel once remarked, "Nothing makes a woman look older than obvious expensiveness and complication." The gracefully aging French woman keeps things simple with her look and her lifestyle. She shops for beautiful accessories, especially scarves that accent her coloring and downplay the signs of age. She chooses bags and luggage carefully, often spending a sizable sum on pieces that will last a lifetime. She selects upscale crockery, glassware, and silver; she sometimes becomes expert in wine or art. Above all, she picks the perfect scent for herself. She may change her perfume with the seasons, as many of the French do (women and men), but the mature woman particularly relies on perfume to enhance her allure. As Coco Chanel said, "A woman without perfume is a woman without a future."

The mature Parisian walks, shops, lunches, dines, and goes to dozens of art shows and exhibitions a year. She drinks sparingly, eats well, and cooks with the freshest ingredients. Madame is also picky about the bottled waters she consumes—and yes, hydrating is a regular tradition in France. Above all, if she can, the ripening Parisian avoids the label of *bouboule* (overweight and dumpy). But this is where the critical function of undergarments comes in (as well as moderate eating.) One of the benefits of exquisite French lingerie is the care with which it's made to enhance any figure. Styles that provide lift and moderate sculpting go a long way toward keeping the maturing French woman looking fabulous like my friend Marie here.

Realistically even the French woman gains a little weight with each advancing decade. But the maturing French woman watches it carefully and accommodates. Writer Ann Morrison commented in "Aging Gracefully, the French Way," published in the *New York Times* in 2010:

"The No. 1 response to my informal survey of Frenchwomen about the years of magical aging is not gaining weight. Ever. If a Frenchwoman happens to see an additional kilogram or two on her bathroom scale, she will do whatever is necessary to force the needle back where it belongs. 'I keep my weight steady, no ups and downs,' Ms. [Leslie] Caron [star of stage and screen] said. 'I avoid all excess.' She claims to eat all kinds of food in small—her friends say minuscule—portions, and she doesn't drink alcohol. It's not so much that 'French Women Don't Get Fat,' as the title of Mireille Guiliano's bestseller had it. Rather, Frenchwomen *won't* get fat."

In her book, *French Women for All Seasons*, Mireille Guiliano, former CEO of champagne maker Veuve Clicquot, analyzes the diet and lifestyle choices of aforementioned Jeanne Calment to find her secrets for longevity. Before she passed at age 122, Calment ate a traditional French-Mediterranean diet of fresh fruits and vegetables, most without pesticides, since few are used in the South of France. She also enjoyed lots of olive oil and small amounts of fresh protein (meats, fish, fowl). She ate the good kind of fats, French cheese, and a glass or two of local red wine or port every day. She ate three meals daily, did not eat fast food, and reportedly savored each bite. She walked and bicycled up to age 100. She was never fat.

Clement was merely one of the many, many older French women who walk with beauty and verve for a very long time. In fact, French women have the longest life expectancy in the Western world except for Japanese women. Today a French woman can expect to live to age 84.32. U.S. women live four years less to age 80.51. Guiliano, herself a handsomely maturing French woman, adds:

"French women traditionally live, as the expression goes, *entre deux âges* (between two ages, or of ambiguous age). Your actual number of years upon the earth is one thing, but after a certain point it is the condition of your mind and body that will dictate your physical and mental age and, by extension, how you feel."

Guiliano suggests that a healthy, disciplined attitude is key to maturing well. And she offers a little psychology to help maintain that discipline. One of the critical areas of control is eating. On average, American women eat 10-30 percent more food than they need each day. One of Guiliano's tricks for eating reasonable proportions the French way is "incrementalism." That is, she recommends eating half or three quarters of something rather than the whole thing. She drinks half a bottle of wine, for example, with her husband at dinner, and then she saves the rest for another meal.

She also splits those scrumptious French desserts with her husband. She counts the number of pieces of a cut baguette that she eats, rather than tearing off a hunk the size of her palm and chowing down without thought. She eats, not drinks, her fruit. She particularly recommends this for Americans, since there's a high probability that bottled and canned juice will contain high-fructose corn syrup—which also appears in many, many other American foods. High-fructose corn syrup may be one of the single most important reasons the average American weight is climbing and diabetes is skyrocketing.

In 2008, 9.1 percent of American women had diabetes. The percentage for French women is well under that, and in 2010 it *fell* by 11 percent! Interestingly, French women also have a far lower diabetes rate than French men. (And judging by the workmen, transportation workers, market staff, and hospitality people around

Paris, I would say that I've seen as many overweight French men as American men.)

Of course, the ripening French woman is also culturally literate and she uses her brain, not just her body. French feminism takes the form of maximizing her potential as a thinking human who also happens to be female. Famous ripening French women abound in the literary, philosophical, and cultural annals of France. None are more famous than Collette. Sidonie-Gabrielle Colette was born in Burgundy but moved to Paris at the age of 20 when she married the music critic and trashy novelist Henri Gauthier-Villars. When the philandering Gauthier-Villars discovered his young bride Colette had charming stories to tell of her sometimes-naughty youth, he used to lock her in her room until she had written enough of them to publish. The Claudine novels were born, which Gauthier-Villars deviously published under his own name.

Later, Colette left him (after she'd cuckolded him with several of his friends). She tried to make a living writing books like *Gigi*, *Renée*, and *Chéri*, but she also had to support herself as a dancer in the Paris music halls. She later had affairs with men and women, and became the toast of Paris in her ripening years. (*Chéri* is her sly book about an aging courtesan who so beguiles a young French aristocrat that he cannot give her up when it's time to wed a young woman who can bear children. It was perhaps more autobiographical than not.)

Colette was smart, sexually liberated, independent, and shrewd. Many say she's the quintessential French woman—and remained so until she died in 1954 at the ripe old age of 81. (Incidentally, in 1951 she happened to see a young, unknown actress walk across the hotel lobby of a southern France hotel. She cried out, "There's my Gigi!" The young actress was cast and played the title role of the Broadway version of *Gigi* for 219 performances. Her name was Audrey Hepburn.)

If there's a way to age well, French women seem successful at doing it. Writer Ann Morrison ("Aging Gracefully, the French Way") describes an elderly woman in her Paris neighborhood that "waltzes down the street to her own imagined music…in a red print skirt, loose cardigan and scarlet cloche…she has great posture and is beautifully made up. She clearly loves being herself. And she makes me think that in France, women might forget everything else as they age—but never their sense of style."

In the words of Coco Chanel, "You can be gorgeous at 20, charming at 40 and irresistible for the rest of your life." French women know a great deal about looking stylish well into their golden years. Some of the secrets of these wise females include the following:

- **Wearing clothes that flatter your particular body shape**. If you have a large bust line like me (that's heading for your knees as you age), learn to minimize it and maximize elsewhere. Long and taut helps avoid a buxom profile.

- **Employ uplifting undergarments**. Yes, we have Spanx now in America that replaces the awful girdles my mother used to wear. But in France, the lingerie is not only practical, it's enthralling as well.

- **Wear clothes with flair by adding eye-catching pins, necklaces, hats, or scarves that provide a signature style**. The French woman evolves a special style that marks her as unique. Chanel had her long necklaces. Ms. France maker Geneviève de Fontenay has her black and white hats. We too can add something to our look that makes us completely unique.

- **Less is more when you're over 50.** These Parisian women cut back on makeup—they don't add more. A little red lipstick can add warmth to the complexion—but a blood-red mouth can make a woman look a lot more like Gloria Swanson than Audrey Tautou. Pinks, corals, apricots all look terrific against a ripening complexion. Subtle colors in nails can also provide a fresh look to mid-life hands.

- **Buy quality.** Peek in the older French woman's closet, and you'll find a few quality pieces in neutrals, rather than a bloated assortment of seasonal pieces from bargain basement emporiums.

- **Invest in classic staples.** These include the Breton Stripe top (horizontal stripes) popularized by Coco Chanel, some well made tees, a chain strap bag, one or two Chanel-esque jackets, a classic trench coat, a blazer, a biker jacket for weekends, a cashmere sweater, a button-down shirt, a few cropped Capri pants, and some skinny jeans, plus some ballet flats and tasteful high heels. All are part of the classic French wardrobe that works no matter your age. And of course never forget to have an LBD (little black dress) in your closet. The right LBD works for a woman of any age.

- **Avoid neon colors unless it's summer.** Neon is too often associated with women struggling to look young. A seasoning woman can add a top or a scarf, of course, to capture the neon shade of the moment. But a whole outfit in day-glow orange can make a female look like a cone at a construction site.

- **Leave mini-skirts and micro-shorts to the girls.** As Inès de la Fressange says in *Parisian Chic,* "No Parisian would ever dress mutton as lamb."

- **Show some skin, but make it age appropriate.** French women who are 50+ and who have great legs can wear the shorter skirts—but certainly not the minis. If they have great arms, they may wear short or no sleeves. If they have beautiful cleavage, they might allow a peek of their beautiful *décolletage.* But not all three at once! Too much skin after 50 is particularly aging; it says you're trying too hard. Classy older women leave something to the imagination; French women especially know the art of subtlety.

- **Avoid leggings.** My daughter can wear them, but when I put on a pair with a tunic I look a little like a pumpkin in a Halloween play. Opt for the full-stocking look.

- **French women avoid flat loafers with dresses and skirts.** They wear them with trousers. A little toe cleavage on a kitten heel works wonders for the middle-age fashionista. Or a classy high heel with a classic dress or suit also works well.

- **Try opaque tights—but in neutral colors.** Also available are the wonderful hosiery you can get in France (and else-where) that dress up an outfit. But French women know to combine colors and textures cautiously. Leopard tights with a leopard scarf and jacket would be too, too much!

- **Shield your face from the sun.** Use a hat, creams, and sunscreen to protect that delicate skin.

- **Heed the 60/40 rule.** Paula Reed's book, *Style Clinic*, suggests that once women hit their 40s, they should have a wardrobe that's 60 percent timeless pieces (trench, white shirt, black pants, cashmere sweater, well-cut blue jeans) and 40 percent trendy wear.

- **Aim for crisp.** Yes, French women iron things so they look fresh. *Le pressing* shops are very busy in Paris. Pressed clothes provide a more classic edge to an overall look. Nothing is more aging than rumpled clothing or misshapen garments that look like we've pulled them from a basket in the closet.

- **Dab from your makeup compact as needed during the day.** Parisians refresh their makeup, especially when their faces look tired.

- **Look after your teeth.** After a certain age, teeth will get stained by red wine, coffee, tea, chocolate, certain fruit, and a variety of other things. A whitened smile goes a long way toward keeping our faces bright and youthful.

- **Avoid blusher applied like war paint, shimmery makeup, too much foundation, and too much mascara.** Lighter is better with maturing skin.

- **Avoid smoking.** Yes, yes, I know. Coco Chanel smoked every day of her life until she died in 1971. By that time, her face looked like a leather saddle left out in the rain. If you don't want to resemble her, stop. Please. (You'll live longer.)

- **Remember these famous words of advice:**

"An hour sleeping or making love is better than a Botox injection at the dermatologist." Inès de la Fressange

"Age does not protect you from love. But love, to some extent, protects you from age." Jeanne Moreau

"A dress makes no sense unless it inspires men to want to take it off you." Francoise Sagan

"Style is knowing who you are, what you want to say, and not giving a damn." Gore Vidal

Parenting

"Where the American child bears the stamp of a certain tempestuous air of privilege and plenty—and the mark of a particular strain of ambivalent permissiveness—the French child is simply the most recent in a long line of progeniture...In France, children don't run the show, adults do. And parenting is one of the rare instances where the French are actually more direct than Americans."

—*Debra Ollivier,* Entre Nous

I had a surreal experience watching French parenting in action one spring in Paris. Printemps, the grand department store, was promoting the movie *Alice in Wonderland* with Johnny Depp. Teatime figured prominently in the story. Printemps had therefore created a wonderland tea salon on the ground floor where shoppers could sip an elegant tea, coffee, or *chocolat* and munch on delicate French pastries.

I sat down to enjoy a cup of mid-morning tea there, and my eyes fell on a French family of four sitting a few feet away. The mid-30s parents were dark haired and handsomely dressed; their two well-turned out children (a boy and girl about five and seven) sat across from them. The entire family was being served tea and pastries, and I watched as the four tucked into their delicious fare.

I tried not to stare, but it was hard not to study what was unfolding before me. These children, dressed in their natty Petit Bateau outfits, sat composed and restrained throughout the entire meal. As an American mother and family therapist who has attempted to do therapy with hundreds of small American children this age who, for the most part, act more like proverbial jumping beans than focused young people, I was mesmerized by the calm before me.

First, I noticed their modulated voices. Second, I noticed there was no wriggling around in their chairs, crumb dropping, or trashing of the area. Third, I observed the practiced way the children used their utensils, expertly cutting up morsels of food and appreciatively chewing them. Last, I was amazed to witness their conversing to their parents, perfectly mirroring their parents' socializing and measured enjoyment of their snacks.

In America, I would've been tempted to deem them "Stepford Children." In fact, they were just French. French children, I've learned, value the dining experience. Acting up is not even in the playbook.

French children are taught very early on that they're expected to behave and will be scolded (or more) if they don't. Strangers, neighbors, and other locals will also scold or coach children as well—and French parents don't typically perceive this as invasive.

It's *expected*. French parents want their children to represent themselves and their families in the most positive light. In France, a parent with misbehaving children is perceived as not having control or
having terrible child-rearing capabilities. A French child that's be-
having well in public is judged *bien élevé* (well-reared). If the child is
misbehaving, French parents bear the brunt of the shame. Societal
control is strong in France; adult behavior is prized, and children
aren't cut any slack just because they're small.

As Gilles Asselin and Ruth Mastron explain in *Au Contraire*:
"The emphasis and locus of control in the United States is the
child. In France, it is the parents." Laurence Wylie further details
the French child's upbringing in *Beaux Gestes: A Guide to French Body
Talk*:

> "By age ten, then, the French children have become bien éle-
> vés (well-reared). They have learned about limits, boundaries,
> delineation, and appropriate behavior...they have learned con-
> trol over themselves, over their bodies. They have acquired
> tremendous inner psychological independence, I think, that
> American children do not have."

The French children I've seen in Paris (and elsewhere in France)
seem self-possessed and polite; they do well with independent play.
At the playground, for example, French parents observe from the
benches; they don't hover over the children. As long as a parent or
adult caretaker is near by, these children behave. There are reports
to the contrary, however, and non-French parents report French
kids seem under-supervised at times. On the other hand, French
parents are critical of American parents for getting too involved
with their children, both in the playground and out. Prominent
in France is the use of *la fessée* (a spank), which would be contro-
versial in America. In fact, there's grumbling even in France that

corporal punishment perhaps plays too big a part in rearing children. This may be one of the dark secrets of well-mannered French children—but I hope not.

Philosophically, French mothers do have some very different ideas about parenting than American mothers. In fact, Pamela Druckerman suggests in *Bringing Up Bébé*: "French mothers love their children as much as anyone, but don't see them as their entire life project, to the exclusion of professional satisfaction, adult leisure time and quality time with a spouse."

Amusingly, even the French government gets involved with the marital satisfaction of new mothers and their partners. The French have a special program called *la rééducation périnéale*, which is part of the postpartum regimen of young mothers in France. It includes 10-20 sessions of state-funded physical therapy (manual and biofeedback) designed to retrain the muscles of the pelvic floor (including the vagina) after childbirth. This may shock some readers, but it's been a government program paid by French Social Security since 1985. It also pays for abdominal re-education that helps *maman's* tummy get back into shape as well. By all reports, the programs are an astounding success.

French mothers are disciplined about themselves; they expect their French children to be just as self-controlled. In the Marais one November, for example, I came across this delightful group of school children (pictured) heading for their *déjeuner* (lunch) down the street at the school "canteen." I could see their teacher to the left; she was the only adult guiding them down the street. They were certainly talking like kids as they walked, but they were orderly and very grown up. The children weren't pushing and shoving; they were controlled and aware of boundaries with each other.

In France, children are also taught moderation. They're not given dozens of toys on birthdays and holidays. They're taught at an early age to be frugal, value their things, and take care of them. They have a structured, adult-centered family life. They grow up learning appropriate boundaries, sitting up at the adult table for meals, eating what the adults eat, and joining in the discourse as soon as they're able.

In "From Baby to Bébé: Learning from French Parenting" on NBCNEWS.com, Pamela Druckerman offers this:

> "The French have managed to be involved without becoming obsessive. They assume that even good parents aren't at the constant service of their children, and that there's no need to feel guilty about this. 'For me, the evenings are for the parents,' one Parisian mother tells me. 'My daughter can be with us if she wants, but it's adult time.' French parents want their kids to be stimulated, but not all the time. While some American toddlers are getting Mandarin tutors and pre-literacy training, French kids are—by design—toddling around by themselves."

French children are particularly reared to value their cultural heritage. Museums, art galleries, and other cultural venues are filled with French families, and the children are generally interested and focused. They eat a wide variety of foods on a regular basis and develop a sophisticated palate from childhood. Many also play a popular board game called *Le Loto des Odeurs* (The Lottery of Smells). This game teaches them to identify dozens of smells like eucalyptus, strawberry, mushrooms, hazelnut, grass, fennel, honeysuckle, and others. The game is foundational for the typical French child to be able to develop a full appreciation of aromas and tastes including the complexities of wine, French cuisine, and extraordinary French perfumes—to name a few.

French children are reared with a sophisticated, well-trained palette. According to Karen le Billon, author of *French Kids Eat Everything*, "the French believe teaching one's children to eat is as important as teaching them to read...from an early age, French children are introduced to a wide variety of foods (e.g., leek soup for babies)." Le Billon, mother of two young daughters, goes on to explain in *France Magazine*, "this 'taste training' is reinforced in the classroom and the lunchroom. The healthy eating routines...also help. For example, no snacking between meals, and no substitutes (i.e., no short order cooking) at mealtime." The author underscores the fact that most French restaurants don't offer children's menus, so children learn to eat what grownups eat—even things like foie gras, bouillabaisse, and mussels.

Schooling is quite rigorous in France. One morning I woke up in my hotel on the Left Bank and looked out my window. Because it was Saturday, I was startled to see children sitting at rows of desks across the street, busily drawing, writing, and doing group work. I soon discovered that French school is held Monday, Tuesday, Thursday, Friday, and often on Saturday mornings. The typical school day in France runs from 8:30 a.m. to 12 noon. The children are given an hour and a half to two hours for lunch, and then they go back to the classroom until 4:30 p.m. In rural areas, children often go home for a three- or four-course luncheon cooked by *leurs mères ou grands-mères* (mothers or grandmothers). Children who can't go home for lunch go to the canteen where they're served a three- or four-course meal (including a starter, main course, dessert, and sometimes a cheese course).

There are few sports or competing interests for a child in a French school. Doing well academically is a French child's main pursuit. They're frequently reminded of the French public education motto that was coined by the 19th century educational reformer Jules Ferry: *"gratuite, obligatoire, et laïque"* (free, compulsory, and secular).

The advancement and acculturation of French children is the keystone of French education. French schools are notoriously difficult, inflexible, competitive, and rigorous. Children are not coddled; they're constantly challenged. Their grades in early school predict their future university education—and often their situation as adults. Where a student's high school grades in America are often forgotten or minimized, especially if the student makes a successful career or garners university accolades later, in France early grades are critical in laying the foundation for a student's life-long position in French society.

French pupils are in school for long hours with lots of homework starting in their young years. On Wednesdays, primary age groups aren't in school. On this day museums, galleries, and exhibits fill with French children. Wednes-days are also days used for music lessons, sporting ac i ities, outings with family like the one pictured, and catechism for young Catholics. After age 11, students attend classes five days a week, often on Saturday mornings as well. Compared to American school children, French children have the longer school day. However, they also have the longest holidays.

The French particularly value the capacity to reason; philosophy is therefore compulsory in French schools until the age of 18. The schooling, especially secondary education, is focused on philosophy regardless of the student's area of specialization. Students are required to pass a module in the subject as part of their baccalaureate before being allowed to go to university. In America, if you talk philosophy and describe yourself as an "intellectual," the image of a beatnik may come to mind. In France, being a cultured intellectual is one of the highest callings.

Parents are focused on their children having the best cultural experience, but a French mother's dictates hold sway. Debra Ollivier explains: "The French mother is often the source of everything that informs the French girl [for example]: a sense of the feminine, of social conduct, poise, etiquette and, of course, cooking. She's an arbiter of continuity and tradition, a sort of magistrate who oversees the smooth functioning of family life—managing conflict, diffusing resentments, letting go of grudges in an elegant and seemingly transparent way."

Taking care of the children is primarily the French woman's job. On back-to-school night only about 15% of the dads are present in private schools; in public schools, the number plummets to about 5%. If there's a problem in the classroom, teachers don't ask to meet the parents; they call Mom's cell phone number directly. However, French parents have plenty of help too. The state offers affordable daycare, free nursery schools, a network of state-subsidized nannies, and cash allocations for every child added to the family. Pediatricians also make house calls!

At school, children aren't pampered and are expected to toe the line. Administrators can be harsh, rather than friendly. And if children get out of line in the neighborhood, neighbors will do a little parenting themselves. In France, personal lawsuits are rare, and people don't hesitate to set children straight if they're acting up.

The children of France have a new advocate, however: President François Hollande. He announced in 2012 that he wants to abolish homework for all primary- and middle-school students. He also wants to shorten the school day and divert more resources to disadvantaged students. His new initiatives may come at a tricky time in French education. Where U.S. students still fall in the lower ranks of education at 17th in the world according to the Economist Intelligence Unit (a division of the company that publishes *The Economist*), the French unfortunately have fallen even further to 25th. But Hollande's reasoning also has a lot to do with equality: he wants to remove the advantage French children have when they have educated, affluent parents who assist them with homework. Hollande feels that underprivileged children have less help and therefore fewer opportunities for success.

I would be very surprised if Hollande's no homework initiative succeeds in France. French children currently do as much as three to four hours of homework at night as a rule—because their parents so adamantly want them to succeed and because the curriculum is so rigorous. (In America, most children do homework for an average of less than an hour a day.) French competition is fierce to score at the top of the class. Unlike America, French grades are posted in public, and class standings are published in the local papers. French parents are quite serious about their children doing well at school. For one thing, they don't want to endure the shame of their children being held back—which happens often in France. Starting at around age 13, low grades may result in the child failing a grade. As a result, French students in their final years of high school may range in age from 16 to 20.

Schools in the U.S. are more inclined to "socially promote" students so they can keep up with their age group—despite their academic failures. (I see many of these academically challenged children in therapy, and they're ashamed to be left behind, but simultaneously they're anxious if they're required to do even more complex work that's over their heads.) In France, the students are given plenty of encouragement or harsh punishment in order to allow them to pass on their own merits. (Punishment seems to dominate.) Students who don't excel academically are pushed into trade schools and relegated to low-level jobs.

Despite the French revolution, France is still rather aristocratic in its conceptualization and enforcement of education. The smartest children are noted and nurtured; the less gifted students are marginalized. There's no such thing as "no child left behind" in France. The goal is to be accepted in one of the *grandes écoles*, institutions of higher learning that aren't state-run schools. Many French corporations recruit directly from these *grandes écoles*, and most politicians have to have a degree from one of them to get anywhere.

French children are also tutored in the art of conversation. Sophisticated discourse is especially important in France; individuals are encouraged to elevate their conversation through discussions of politics, food, wine, and philosophy, rather than mundane topics like weather and finances. The exchange of opinions is critically important; school children are taught throughout their education how to reason and analyze a topic from different viewpoints. They learn not to take intellectual differences personally. Oral exams are also part of their test regimen. And oral discourse continues at home and in public. Americans watching French people talking in a *café* are sometimes struck by how much the French will expound on a topic, for example. Then they are shocked by how much the French speakers interrupt each other, openly arguing, but then leave later, all smiles.

While the educational system is exacting, my sense is that French children grow up to be a bit more well-rounded and academically accomplished than many American children. But this is up for debate. One fierce critic of the French education system is Pascal-Emmanuel Gobry. Gobry, who is French, writes in *The Atlantic* about his loathing for the way French children are educated and reared. He flatly posits: "The way French education works, and I don't know if I could put it in a more charitable way, is that it seeks to mercilessly beat any shred of nonconformity out of children (the beating is now done mostly psychologically) so that they may be slotted into a society that, itself, treats nonconformity the way the immune system treats foreign elements." He goes on to say that as a parent he's considering putting his own daughter into a Montessori school or homeschooling rather than putting her through a French education.

Views differ.

Like most countries, there are probably good and bad elements to French parenting. I do admire the aplomb of the French children I've seen, however. And, in the words of my French friend Marie-Geneviève, "In France, we have the legacy of Voltaire, the

artistry of Chanel, and the pre-eminence of French cuisine. Our children are not perfect—and neither are we as parents—but I can think of a lot worse places to grow up than in the shadows of the Eiffel or across the Seine from Notre Dame (pictured)."

Fraternity

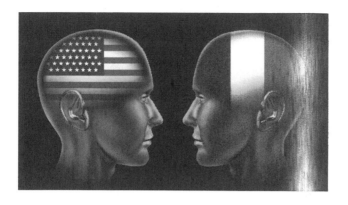

"When good Americans die they go to Paris."
—Oscar Wilde, *A Woman of No Importance* (1893)

Some Americans love France. Others loathe the difficult language, the sometimes insolent citizens, and the cultural snobbery that clouds the French psyche like some kind of Louis XIV fog. Likewise, some French people adore America and can't wait to go there. Other French citizens hope never to set foot in the U.S. bastion of over-commercialization, freeway congestion, and overbearing Americanism.

Two strong cultures. Two fervent world powers. Very different approaches to lifestyle, commerce, government, philosophy, and psychological angst.

Despite the obvious differences, I'd suggest these two cultures have much in common, yet plenty to learn from their disparate perspectives. My friend Marie-Geneviève is a case in point. She's an effervescent French woman in her 40s who came to America about 15 years ago. Now a mother of two who works as a graphic designer for an American publishing company, Marie says she takes from American culture what works for her. "But I never give up my French ideals. Americans are kind of rough around the edges. Friendly at first. Sometimes fierce about what they want and how they expect to get it. Some of them treat outsiders like *imbéciles*. France is more contained—but we can be snobs too. We're just more subtle about it. I agree we French have our own way of doing things. We don't trust people at first like you cheery Americans. Yes, our opinions can be sharp. But when we disagree, we talk and then kiss and go to dinner. *C'est vrai.* You Americans carry the big stick—and use it."

The French have their stereotypes of America just as Americans have preconceived notions of France. Some French people see Americans as wealthy, arrogant, and domineering. They see us pushing toward the future at the speed of light. Many Americans see the French languishing in the past, moldering like the walls of Versailles with an aging patina that gets harder and harder to maintain without modern intervention.

Philosophically, these are two proud cultures that seem to believe their way is best. Each is steeped in its own unique brand of ferocious history, hard-won freedoms, and psychological victories. Emotionally, from my view, the two cultures can be equally as unforgiving if their boundaries are infringed. But each can be disarmingly gracious to strangers too if the conditions are right. Despite the veneer of occasional intractability, I'd suggest that the people of France and the people of America share a common core of conviviality and commitment to family values.

Still, France preens a bit. And America likes to crow about its mighty deeds. Ergo as birds of a different feather, they don't necessarily flock together. *Le Coq*, the French rooster, is one of the most famous mascots of France. The eagle is an icon of America, revered for its majestic freedom and strength. But feathers may fly, as Gilles Asselin and Ruth Mastron point out in *Au Contrairie! Figuring Out the French*, when the eagle comes beak to beak with *Le Coq* of the walk.

> "The rooster is to the French what the bald eagle is to Americans. Yet a rooster does not fly high in the sky, and it does not soar to reach high peaks and discover new horizons. Rather, a rooster wakes up the entire village at dawn, attracts attention from others, and never retreats from his defiant and domineering attitude toward the rest of the coop. Nowadays, French influence is certainly not as far-reaching as it used to be, and the world is much larger and more complex than a single coop. Still, some French roosters like to remind everyone that France has awakened the entire world to the beauty and grace of its civilization, culture, and language."

These are generalizations, of course. Many are based on superficial interactions or media-framed caricatures. But the reality is that two people meeting in Place de Vosges in the Marais are just two human beings, though one may be French and one may be American. Their common bond is humanity—and their desire to connect.

But nobody said it's easy.

Alexis de Tocqueville wrote in 1865 that "the French are both the most brilliant and most dangerous of all European nations, and the best qualified to become, in the eyes of other peoples, an object of admiration, hatred, compassion, or alarm—never of indifference." I agree it's hard to be indifferent about the French. They're colorful, opinionated, romantic, difficult, charming, and well, French. But it's all in the willingness to risk having the one-on-one experiences with them that we Americans can find the richness of common ground, I believe.

Face-to-face, in the domestic day-to-day, we see the flesh and blood of real life, whether it's on American soil or French—and can judge for ourselves. Those of us who seek foreign travel do so probably because we desire a multi-cultural experience. But cultural intimacy evolves when we leave caution on the tarmac and freely allow ourselves to participate in a new cultural experience, good and bad.

That's the France I see when I go there, live there. Marie says that's the America she experiences in the U.S. "I certainly enjoy my children being in American schools, but I cook *coq au vin* at home and watch soccer at night with them on my American television; I feel good that they're getting a varied experience. We take what we like from both countries."

Still, the French can be hard to "read" at times. They don't seem to be un-American exactly. I believe they're conflicted. While many French people criticize American commercialism and globalization, they openly love American music, American movies, and American technology. When I get into a taxi and hear Bruce Springsteen or Beyoncé on the radio, I'll sometimes ask the taxi driver why he plays American music. He'll usually smile and says something like: *"Parce que ça nous plaît."* ("Because we like it.") When I pull out my iPhone in a Parisian *café*, I see dozens of other French people scanning Facebook or answering email on their iPhones as well. They look at me approvingly.

Despite some grumbling in l'Hexagone, the U. S. is still a very popular tourist destination for many French people. As of this writing more than one million French people even make the U.S. their home. Five percent of Paris is made up of resident Americans. American books, television programs, and films continue to be a huge influence in France. French actor Jean Dujardin's recent Academy Award for best actor in *The Artist* also demonstrates the allure of Hollywood for France and French entertainers.

I sat next to a French honeymooning couple on a flight from Paris to Los Angeles last year. The wife spoke perfect English. But her new husband cowered in his seat next to the window, afraid to open his mouth since he spoke not one word of English. She told me they were stopping by Hollywood for a few days on their honeymoon, then they were travelling on to Tahiti. "We want to see the Sunset Strip," she offered. I cautioned her that Hollywood and Vine isn't necessarily representative of America as a whole—and to "watch out for all the strange people in heavy makeup and exotic costumes."

Her husband's eyes practically bugged out of his head when she translated what I'd said. My heart went out to him. Here was a strapping, handsome French husband going to America—and completely dependent on his wife to take him there among the savages of Hollywood. Fear and attraction often go hand-in-hand when we venture out into the cultural wilds. I can relate.

Still, the American allure is catnip to many of the people of France. The outrageous largesse. The cocky confidence. The big, the brash, the bold. One thing I know about the French is that they admire *panache*—even if it's not their own. And of course the country of France offers much to Americans that's some combination of cultural mystique, enviable style, culinary sophistication, and just plain seduction. The French army may not be as large as America's, but there's a powerful French brigade of seducers (cultural, culinary, and sexual) that have infiltrated the world's psyche as a force to be reckoned with. Caesar may have proclaimed: "I came, I saw, I conquered." But the French could claim with equal audacity: "I welcomed, I flirted, I seduced." And how.

Nonetheless there's psychological resistance between the American bazooka and the French *baguette*. One of these areas of friction is in commerce. The French remain conflicted about creeping American commercialism on their own soil, for example. They've resisted certain American "intrusions" like Euro Disney. It's one thing to visit Hollywood. It's another to find Mickey and his pals holed up just outside the City of Light

The French didn't buy it at first. When the sprawling Mickey Mouse Fantasy Park located east of Paris in Marne-la-Vallée opened its door in 1992, the French complained. Legions of angry protestors marched against the park that represented the over-commercialization of all things American. Disney finally had to launch its own charm offensive. It bowed to French preferences and added wine and French food to the park's menu. Later, the name was even changed to Disneyland Paris. But by recent accounts, only 50% of the park's visitors are French. (I once sat next to a boisterous family of five from Dublin, Ireland who had flown into Paris just to take the train out to Disneyland for the weekend. They loved the park, but they told me: "We don't much care for the French!")

Despite French grumbling, American consumerism steadily spreads into Paris. You can find a McDonald's (*McDo* in French) and Starbuck's within walking distance of most any Parisian hotel. If American visitors tire of *bœuf bourguignon*, they can wander over to McDo and chow down on *le McBaguette* (burger on a French *baguette*), *le Royal Deluxe* (cheeseburger), or *Le Big Mac* (with two patties).

According to many unhappy French farmers, however, McDonalds is a symbol of the proliferation of *la malbouffe* (bad eating) taking over their country. They may be right. But currently, France is also coming to terms with a precarious European Community, where certain nations (Germany and France) are having to bail out troubled countries (Greece, Portugal, and others) as the economic downtown rolls over Europe like a tsunami. France needs tourism and American corporate resources—and despite the fact that some French people hold their noses, they take American dollars because they need them.

America went through its economic contraction from 2008-2013 and now seems on the rise again. But France is still undergoing economic wrangling with the rest of the European Union, as well as some internal feuding between the wealthy French who don't want to pay 75% taxes and the rest of the citizenry who demand the government coffers pay for their French pensions and social services. As of this writing, even millionaire French actor Gérard Depardieu has announced he'll pay no more taxes to the country of his birth. He's left France in a *pique* and set up house in Belgium just across the border from France. He's allegedly renounced his French citizenship. (Belgium has a top income tax rate of 50% and doesn't levy capital gains tax on share transactions nor does it have a wealth tax like France.) Depardieu is even eyeing a Russian passport.

Across the pond, French people doing business in America are often shocked at our low tax rates and how stoically American business unfolds. Take cocktails for example. In America, more of the fine details of a deal are worked out over cocktails or at the beginning of a meal. Time is money in America, and the food is not to be enjoyed until after the hard work is done. Work before pleasure.

On French soil, the opposite occurs. The ritual of multicourse dining creates a space for hours of wining and dining that builds rapport over shared pleasure. It all climaxes in sealing the deal over coffee. In France, business is typically discussed only after the main dish has been served and eaten. When *poire et le fromage* (pear and cheese) appears, the true business discussions begin. Americans conducting business in France have to wait patiently for that right moment of satiety to close the deal. Then and only then will the

French businessperson get to the work at hand. Pleasure before work.

In France, living one's life in the pursuit of pleasure is considered civilized. Work is a means to an end—the enjoyment of the fruits. With their five to six weeks of vacation a year versus the American two to three week dash to relax, the French demand their vacation time and make time to do nothing (in Italy it's called *il dolce far niente*, the "sweetness of doing nothing").

French people may become entrepreneurs, but until success strikes, an "entrepreneur" in France is usually someone desperate. He or she is a sap, rebelling against the viability of France's venerable institutions of solidarity, fraternity, and equality that provide lifetime support from early employment to retirement and beyond.

In the U.S., the successful entrepreneur is king. He or she is an adventurer who strikes out to conquer the jungles of American commerce. There may be spoils—but the real prize is more work. Work *is* the reward. The busier the better. The American may even be suspicious of too much pleasure—since it may soften his or her edge.

Another area of difference is personal consumption. French people and American people spend quite differently. Americans tend to buy quantity rather than quality. In France, a few high-end purchases are preferred that will last a lifetime rather than many low-end acquisitions that fall apart from wear or cheap workmanship. Artisan quality is highly valued in France. Quality is certainly valued in America, but typically only a small percentage of the population will be able to afford it; the cash poor will opt for cheaper choices or knock-offs. Stores still close in France on Sundays for time with family; often they're closed on Monday as well. In America, even if our favorite big-name store is closed, online retailers will still be able to ship anytime, day or night.

Personal finances are also managed differently in France than America. It's considered vulgar to advertise one's wealth in France. The French are busier hiding their wealth than flaunting it. Of course, there is "bling" in France. But most of it is in hallowed places like Versailles and the Louvre or sequestered behind gated compounds in the south of France. The French tend to live within their means, save rigorously, and avoid using credit. They invest in homes, second homes, boats, art, quality home goods, and upscale wardrobes with a limited number of very good pieces. They distrust the stock market and get-rich-quick schemes.

In America, investors generally trust the stock market and other investments to grow their wealth. They hire financial advisors to get the best return in the shortest amount of time. They take risks to realize high return. The French don't like risks in general. And they particularly don't like putting someone else in charge of their future (except the government, which is more like *mon père* than big brother). Since they mistrust the stock market they think Americans are daft for putting their life savings into it.

Politically, America and France also have a rather love-loathe perspective on how things should be done. When the twin towers tumbled in 2001, Jean-Marie Colombani of *Le Monde* newspaper declared: "We are all Americans now." But when the U.S. invaded Iraq soon after, the French sneered with disapproval. In response, Americans stopped eating French fries for a time and boycotted French wine. "Yes," Marie tells me, "Americans can dig their heels in just like we French can."

But France and America also share a certain political arrogance. France hasn't been a real military or political power since the 19th century. According to Elaine Sciolino in *La Seduction*:

"Since [Napoléon], [France] has had to rely more on powers of persuasion. In the years since World War II, France has had to adapt to its stature as a relatively minor power, learning how and when to woo the wider world. France is too weak an economic and military power to counterbalance the United States but too strong and too strong-willed to take orders from it. In addition, it has to compete with two sets of powers: established ones like the United States, Russia, and China, and emerging ones like Brazil and India, whose strength and potential on many fronts are greater than its own...In a permanent wound to its pride, it has lost one of its most powerful weapons—the supremacy of the French language, which long ago ceased to be the language of international diplomacy."

France has had to temper its colonizing philosophy called *mission civilisatrice* (civilizing mission). But on some level, America has a similar zeal to "liberate" areas of the globe and ergo impart (some say "inflict") American ideals and values onto foreign people. Without wading too far into political quicksand here, I see a parallel zeal between France and America, which strut (and have strutted) their stuff for the world to "gratefully" embrace.

Who wouldn't be tempted to run from the heavy boots of French or American ethnocentrism?

Interestingly, the Statue of Liberty is a philosophical and political link between the two countries that graphically demonstrates some of our shared ideology. I was strolling through the Left Bank's Luxembourg Gardens one day when I came around a tree-lined pathway and saw this familiar sight:

Yes, this is Lady Liberty—in Paris. She stands erect and proud in the lush gardens near the Sorbonne. How did she come to be in Paris of all places?

When sculptor Frédéric Auguste Bartholdi, the son of Italian immigrants who settled in France, first saw New York Harbor in 1871, he became a man with a mission.  Seeking places to display his work, he had recently joined the Union Franco-Américaine, which sought in 1870 to model the New France after America upon the fall of the repressive Napoléon III regime. The French had already established strong ties during the American War of Independence when France was a crucial ally (and supplied barrels of money). Crafting a work of art that would herald not only the centennial of American independence, but act as a beacon for the new, independent France became Bartholdi's calling.

Bartholdi's idea was to create a colossal statue based on *Libertas*, the Roman goddess of liberty. The undertaking took fundraising on both sides of the Atlantic and required nine years of building. Finally, she was erected on Bedloe's Island (now Liberty Island), the site Bartholdi had selected nearly 15 years before. It was officially dedicated on Oct. 28, 1886. She stands today at 305 feet 1 inch—about 22 stories high.

In 1889, Bartholdi erected a 40-foot replica of Lady Liberty on the Île aux Cygnes, an island in the River Seine. The France version holds a tablet bearing the dates of the American Independence Day and France's July 14 (Bastille Day). And finally, the small bronze that Bartholdi used to create his massive original found a home in the lovely Luxembourg Gardens among the proud statuary. It was this one I encountered in the gardens that day. I was touched to find Lady Liberty standing before me in Paris—and I felt the umbilical cord of shared ideals connecting me not only to America in that moment, but to France as well in some small way.

France and America share this noble idea of freedom and liberty for all. Thomas Jefferson, recognized in Europe as the crafter of the Declaration of Independence, even became a symbol for revolutionaries in Europe. Some say Jefferson's writings influenced France's *Declaration of the Rights of Man* approved by the National Assembly of France in 1789. The wording is eerily similar to the American Declaration of Independence, proclaiming that men are born free and equal in rights. (See the remnants of the French Revolution in today's Carnavalet Museum in the heart of the Marais District, where you'll find a copy of the Declaration and even remnants of the rope ladders the revolutionaries used to climb over the walls of the Bastille. Or check out the Pantheon where many of the great leaders of France are buried. One of the marvelous pillars is depicted here.)

Philosophically, France and America have much in common. But they also have different ways of interpreting their own ideals. Where America relies heavily on the concept of independence *à la* the Declaration of Independence, France relies heavily on the notion of *liberté, égalité, fraternité* (liberty, equality, fraternity) with a dogged emphasis on *fraternité*—togetherness.

In America, the power of the individual can move a mountain. Hence our icons tend to be solitary men and women like Davy Crockett, Orville Wright (and his brother), Teddy Roosevelt, Amelia Earhart, John D. Rockefeller, and Steve Jobs who fought the good fight, built an industry, or changed the world, largely with individual persistence.

France is maintained more by the power of the people. "French solidarity" is a phrase that's often used. It means banding together to fight for what's right for the whole. The collective is more important and more powerful than the individual. Street protests are one of the manifestations of the French spirit of solidarity. The French value their independence and refuse to be cowed by kings, government, businesses, or any other authority. They make their wishes known, particularly through street protests, which actually look to me a lot more like street parties than angry marches.

One of the most memorable examples occurred in April 2010 when more than 1,200 farmers from all around France entered Paris in their immaculate tractors for a defiant drive around the capital. They were escorted by police motorbikes, of course, and watched by millions as they made their way through Paris protesting the precipitous drop in wheat prices. "And how," they cried, "if we are bankrupt and can't grow wheat, will the bakers be able to bake *baguettes*?!" Soon, the bakers shuttered their *boulangeries* and marched along with them—with half of Paris joining in.

As for modern-day politics, Americans, in general, tend to see government as a necessary evil. (But in the downturn economy over the last five years, Americans have been very willing to ask for governmental assistance.) In France, French citizens pay enormous taxes compared to Americans. But they, in turn, expect governmental assistance cradle to grave. There's no shame in this in France. It is *de rigueur.* If the citizenry sees the government or its officials getting out of line or becoming too westernized like former head of France Nicholas Sarkozy (Président Bling-Bling), the French vote them out of office.

On a psychological level, I also detect some amusing differences between the citizens of France and America. One of them is disposition. David Lebovitz recounts in *The Sweet Life In Paris:*

> "One of the first words I learned in French class was *râleur*, which means 'someone who complains.' Maybe it's *la grisaille*, the dull, gray skies that hang over Paris, causing *la morosité ambiente*, the all-encompassing gloom that blankets the city at times. Complaining is such an important part of life here that my first French teacher felt it's a word we needed to learn right off the bat."

In a recent Gallup poll, French people scored among the unhappiest people on the planet. And, according to the *Barometer of Hope and Despair* (that's a doozy of a title for an assessment, isn't it?), the French came in as the global champions of negativity. The assessment for 2012 economic prosperity/difficulty reported the French assessed at a minus 80% in net hope. The U.S. only scored minus 21 despite our economic downturn, slow housing recovery, and high unemployment. (Even Afghanistan only scored a minus four with Iraq scoring a plus 26—quite optimistic!) Despite their long lives, their long vacations, their national health, and their sublime cuisine, the French are still the grumps of the world. (Notice

these two I snapped on Rue Cler. No wonder they ring every second out of their two-hour meals!)

The irritable French have a hard time understanding the mostly sunny disposition of Americans. "In Paris," Olivier Magny writes in *Stuff Parisians Like,* "enthusiasm is considered a mild form of retardation. If you are happy, you must be stupid. On the other hand, if you complain, you must be smart." Much of what Olivier writes is tongue-in-cheek of course. But some of this negativism may simply be a French defense mechanism. To me, the French may be snarky simply to protect themselves. If they're a bit cynical at first, then they can't be too disappointed later. Americans tend to open themselves up right away—and the French think some of us are chumps.

But then there's *French ennui*, roughly equivalent to moderate dysthymia in America (mild depression over two years). *Ennui*, or discontented weariness, is a French condition that somehow seems to be part of the French soul. This attitude of existential despair threads through much of French literature, philosophy, and entertainment. The French ask themselves: Who am I? What am I? How am I known? How do I know myself?

French philosopher René Descartes ventured an answer to these age-old questions with his Cartesian body of rational thought. His philosophical pearl (in Latin), *"Cogito ergo sum"* ("I think, therefore I am"), was supposed to offer peace to the existential mind. But today's French man or woman still seems a bit pensive, even pessimistic. This may be one of the reasons for the preoccupation with dead people in Paris. At various cemeteries like Père Lachaise cemetery in the 20th arrondissement, the living French visit graveyards like they're adventure parks. And, in the subterranean tunnels and caverns of Paris, stuffed with French skeletons and skulls, there are even guided tours day and night. I'm not a skeletal voyeur myself. I go to France for the living. But the abundance of French dead in common sight perhaps contributes to a certain French fatalism.

Americans are generally perceived as more hopeful, despite our phobias, obsessions, and fondness for reality television. (Interestingly, the French *Survivor* program had its first death among the contestants. As far as I know there've been no American casualties, so far.) The emotional makeup of Americans vs. the French couldn't be more at odds.

One of my favorite films highlighting the friction between the French and American psyche is the 1995 movie *French Kiss*. Meg Ryan plays an obsessive, but hope-driven American in pursuit of her lost *fiancé*. Kevin Kline plays a shady, cynical French thief in pursuit of funds to rebuild a vineyard. The two psyches play against each other as the pair journey from Paris to the South of France. Ryan's character eventually confronts Kline's low self-esteem and underhanded methods. In turn, Kline's character lifts out of his funk long enough to "turn the light on" in Ryan by acknowledging her beauty within and without. Of course they're a match made in Cannes (French heaven), a perfect blend of American tenacity and French verve where love conquers all.

Emotionally, however, Americans and the French sometimes disconnect from the get go—and stay that way. Americans are quick to bond, but slow to connect at a deeper level. We greet each other like long-lost relatives everywhere we go (which may be one of the reasons they like to seat Americans together at French restaurants.)

But the French perceive all this instant bonding as suspect. The French are slow to warm. They take their time getting to know someone. Oh, they will be cordial, but only if you observe their local customs first (*Bonjour, Merci, S'il vous plaît*) and wait your turn. They'll only become truly friendly if they think they can trust you, and if you're going to be around for a while to make a positive contribution to their lives or their culture.

I can understand their reticence.

America has never been overrun by a foreign power. But France has. Several times. The evidence of the Roman invasion lies everywhere in France, for example. From Roman roads to Roman aqueducts to Roman baths, the French had their terrain and their culture infiltrated by the pesky Italians—and many of them even settled down to stay in Provence ("the Provinces"). In recent history, the French have had to negotiate around surly invaders like Hitler and the Third Reich. But the French triumphed—and Hitler did not.

France seems to have mastered a well-honed diplomatic finesse that maintains its culture in the face of truly frightening interlopers. Some nations might call the French weak or opportunistic. I would call them survivors.

Today, the French downplay the negatives in their history—or turn them into positives through reframes. (Americans are very good at doing that, as well.) The Carnavalet Museum devotes entire rooms to the French Revolution and the destruction of French royalty, for example, while in the courtyard outside stands a splendid statue of Louis XIV, whom the French revere, despite the fact they guillotined his progeny.

Even Marie Antoinette has been turned into a "princess, icon, rebel" as described by the Paris newspaper *Le Figaro*. When Sofia Coppola was allowed unprecedented access to Versailles to film her $40 million film *Marie Antoinette*, all of France reveled in the "misunderstood, decapitated Marie Antoinette, the remorse of the French."

The French are conflicted about their history. According to Elaine Sciolino in *La Seduction*, "the French are at once stuck in their past and charmed by their national stories and myths…few seem troubled that a permanent obsession with monarchy coexists so easily with the ideals of the Republic."

Likewise in America, we tend to conveniently dismiss the hardship we brought to the Native American people as part of the quest for expanding the new America. But this is part of the cultural drive France and America share—a powerful quest to colonize and impart our ways of living—sometimes at the expense of people with lesser power who were there first. Both France and America are good at reframing events to put themselves in the best light.

France and America can both be fickle on the other hand. Despite their self-proclaimed solidarity, for example, the French are masters at manipulating the system. (And the system even lets them.) Ethics are handled differently in France. Ethics tend to be applied contextually, rather than across the board. The French tend to enjoy "getting around the system" and honor anyone who can figure out how to do it. That's one of the reasons the French reportedly hate the tax collector and why they hide how much money they make. In America we might label this tax fraud; in France they call it cleverness. In America we frown on tax evasion and business fraud, but during the recent credit default swap debacle, very few perpetrators actually went to jail.

"Telling the French that something is not allowed is a direct challenge to their ability to do it gracefully finding an elegant way of bypassing the rules and not getting caught," says Asselin and Mastron. This may be one of the reasons there's so much dog poop on the streets of Paris. Parisians know there's a law that prohibits their little Fifis from defiling the streets, but many of them ignore it.

This is also one of the reasons I would describe the French temperament as mercurial. That is, the French swing between liberal and conservative, free-wheeling and rigid, playful and despairing. Looking out the window of my rented Paris apartment one morning, I saw this site (pictured).

I loved this existential blend of art and ennui. It's so like the French to use something modern like post-it notes to broadcast a message of contemplation.

What's it all about, André?

I wonder if the French psyche is stuffed with competing feelings about the future and the past, wherein mini cars glide by golden chariots and bottles of Grand Cru drift alongside teen liters of Mountain Dew. Interestingly, the French have even provided the psychological profession with some of its most bizarre psychological diagnoses. *Folie à deux* is one of them.

Folie à deux literally means "madness for two." It refers to a shared delusion that's transmitted from one individual to another. It can be a shared belief in a common persona. Examples are bank robber couples (what I call the "Bonnie & Clyde syndrome") or tandem delusions like fearing alien invasions, causing a couple to board up their home and prepare for Armageddon.

As a peculiar cultural collision between this psychosis and wine in America, I cite the story of a California winery in Napa based on the delusion. *Folie à deux* was a winery launched by a pair of married psychologists who decided to pour their conjugal savings into wine. The label evolved into a hot property. Alas, the couple's personal chemistry fizzled. They divorced, madness gone, and the wine label was sold to another Napa bottler who presumably absorbed the name without taking on the psychosis.

Jolie laide is another French concept that illustrates the French tendency toward psychological ambiguity. It means "beautiful ugly." *Jolie laide* encourages embracing the opposites that inevitably occur in relationships. This love-hate dynamic is seen throughout French relationships, books, and movies, as well as in cultural interactions. (*Jolie laide* is probably another reason why cultural friction between France and America is both annoying and invigorating. Without Americans, whom would the French have to complain about?)

The French believe they're centuries ahead of America in experience and wisdom. And they like to remind America of this important heritage. Like an elder dog and a puppy, France has the perspective of time and patience, while America has the enthusiasm of a young culture with plenty of pep as well as bite.

I agree we Americans have a childlike hope about us. We're surprised when other cultures rebuff us. But the French are distrustful of this golly-gee aspect of our culture; I suspect they see us as emotionally *naïve*. Americans do tend to see the glass two thirds full, while the French only perceive a shot at the bottom of that glass. Take this popular Paris slogan, for instance, depicted in the photo.

In English, this means, "I love Nothing...I'm Parisian." Parisians are known for being especially cynical. When I've traveled in the French countryside, even the suburban French say Parisians are cantankerous.

But then there are the wonderful kindnesses of the compassionate French. Like the time my American friends Barbara and Rick, who spoke no French, were wandering around Paris in the late evening looking for the *métro*. While the pair was standing under a street lamp trying to decipher a Paris map, a nicely dressed elderly Parisian man stepped toward them and asked if they needed help. After some back and forthing, the kind man literally took the pair by the hand and led them down to the *métro*—and even handed them a *métro* pass so they could get on the train!

Yet the French can get impatient with American impatience. The ambling French pace drives some Americans crazy—especially at airports, in customs lines, or with anything involving permits, approvals, or contracts.

Nowhere is there more cultural disconnect than in the day-to-day lives of the French vs. Americans. Americans rush. The French *flâner*. *Flâner* means to stroll along, taking your time while daydreaming, having no particular agenda. This is a long-held tradition in France; thus you will see many Parisians, calmly sitting in Paris, nurturing a *café crème*, watching the world go by. The French believe this national pastime of *flâner* is very important as a state of philosophical reverie wherein new perceptions of one's self, one's associates, and one's world can spring forth.

The French think Americans act in haste—and by association, don't think or feel very deeply. But many Americans do want to slow down, to reflect. They go to France specifically to *flâner*—even if they don't call it that. They go to wander along the Champs Élysée. To stroll along the Seine watching the barges drift by. To saunter through the Louvre with no particular agenda and then stop in at a street *café* for a sip of wine—even if it's at 10 am as in this photo above.

Then there's sex. Legions have been written about the differences between American and French perspectives on lovemaking (see chapter titled *Passion*). Suffice it to say, the French are fairly free with nudity, marital and extra-marital sex, and love in general. They're more accepting of people's bodies, no matter their age, and they value the human form. They especially love naturalness—and don't fret over imperfections.

Americans, on the other hand, are more self-conscious about nudity and sex. We're hesitant and secretive—which the French find amusing. The French make love more as part of a relationship rather than as a fling. The mistress or gigolo has a certain standing in France—some are even accepted into the family. Americans, of course, have trouble with all this guiltless frolicking—but they seem to enjoy watching it (and sometimes participating in it.)

Strangely, France and America reverse themselves when it comes to personal privacy. Americans love to Facebook, Tweet, and blog about themselves. (There's even part of that need to disclose in this book!) But in France, one of the most prized values is privacy. They keep shutters on their homes, for example, not only against the cold but to keep their business private. The French are stunned to see our open bay windows in America, where passersby can look in to see the family eating dinner, watching television, or absorbed in other pursuits.

The French are guarded. They don't talk much about their personal lives outside their immediate friends or family. When someone is arrested or caught being naughty, the media doesn't advertise their predicament (although even some of that is changing). And the personal lives of famous and political French people are generally respected. This could be one of the many reasons famous Americans like Jackie Kennedy or Olivia de Havilland decamp to France for the privacy.

C'est la vie, the French would say. It's life, simply life. Americans who enjoy the French life style will find much to love and learn in France. French travellers in America will likewise find an abundance of joys and challenges in the United States of diversity. But I think Gilles Asselin and Ruth Mastron in *Au Contraire* framed it best.

> "It is no accident...that one of the great masterpieces of American art is Grant Wood's *American Gothic,* showing a stern-faced farmer and his daughter in front of their farmhouse. The father holds a pitchfork. These people clearly have work to do and are serious about it. It is no accident either that one of the great French masterpieces is Rodin's *The Thinker*, a statue of a man sitting and thinking."

Perhaps it's true that Americans *do* while the French *think*. But what a sublime confection we can create if we resolve to do our doing and thinking together. *Vive la différence!*

Sociability

Yes, they speak French in Paris.

But it was not always the case. The area known as France has passed through many language iterations on the way to the modern-day *langue Français.* Those pesky Romans brought along Latin when they invaded the French provinces, but the Celts, Franks, and a variety of other interlopers left behind words and place names, seeding the local tongue with bits of foreign language DNA. In fact, the original Parisii tribe, who inhabited central Paris, was a Celtic community that established a fishing village on the Seine River. Later, their name morphed into the Paris *sobriquet* we know and love today.

Slowly, the cacophony of sounds transformed into an elegant (but tongue challenging) language. By the 13th century, French was spreading throughout Europe as the language of sophistication. It became the vernacular of peacemaking, preferred by countries opting to negotiate rather than long-sword each other while shouting, *"Merde, vous méchants étrangers, prends ca!"* ("Damn you nasty foreigners, take that!")

In 1453, the end of the Hundred Years' War marked another huge boost for the French language, which gained strength as the parlance of diplomats despite efforts by the English to stomp it out altogether. (Today many Americans struggling to order coffee with cream in a Paris *café* may feel the English were on to something.) By the 17th century, however, French held sway as the world's most popular language for international relations.

The esteemed Académie Française, established in 1635, convened to oversee the use of French in commercial and workplace communications. Today it still operates, dubbing things male (*le chien*—dog) or female (*la vache*—cow) and attempting to expel anything unFrench from the language (like the word *computer,* which they instead insist on calling *l'ordinateur,* although you often see the word "computer" on French websites anyway). The Académie Française is sort of the "language police"; they consider it a very important duty to maintain the integrity of the French language.

But there are still some moments of consternation from tourists. Visitors sometimes feel they're marginalized if they don't speak any French. Some Americans complain they're even mistreated when the people of France don't automatically begin speaking English to them.

Believe me, I've been there. This language divide can lead to misunderstandings and even escalating conflict. But there are ways to learn about French language customs to smooth the way for cultural harmony. This includes learning a bit of French—or at least comprehending a little of what is communicated and expected by the French natives.

Still, English speakers have trouble with the vocabulary and the accent. This is despite the fact that French has seeped into everyday English in places like Tallahassee and Newark. You'll hear Americans talking about *derrières, couture,* and *croissants* without giving it much thought. And in Paris, despite the fierce oversight of the language *gendarmes,* American-speak has slipped into French conversations about *le feedback, le scotch (tape), la RAM,* and even that place to grab a drink, *le bar.* Hilariously, I even encountered this sign at the Boulevard Raspail Market on the Left Bank.

That's pure English, folks. They were touting cheap French wines, but they were still able to reach out to the language-challenged English-speaking tourists and assure them in English that the wine in the box wasn't bilge.

Still, English speakers can get a bit uppity (read: entitled) in Paris about the language differences. I recently read in Karen Henrich's *Practical Paris* that she finds many visitors are surprised that French is still predominantly spoken in France. And that the street signs in Paris are in French as well! (*Quelle surprise!*) She patiently reminds readers that many of the service people speak *some* English, but often outside the tourist areas, the French tend to stick to French.

Ergo, if you're going to spend time in the City of Light, you may want to learn some rudimentary phrases and understand how to use the French niceties. I'm not suggesting one has to be fully fluent, but to understand a few cardinal rules of French language etiquette will go a long way toward making your Paris stay more pleasant. For example, saying *"bonjour monsieur"* or *"bonjour madame"* to personnel you meet in shops, restaurants, or other public places is expected. When I first began visiting Paris, I was shy about speaking French and so I would avoid the shop personnel whenever I could. But this backfired: I think they regarded me as suspicious as a result. They were decidedly unhelpful when I only spoke English to them when I needed something.

Now, I've learned to say *"bonjour"* (hello) whenever I enter a shop and *"merci"* (thanks) or *"au revoir"* (goodbye) when I leave. There's a cultural imperative here. The French see their shops and places of business as an extension of their homes; they consider it rude to enter and exit without addressing the niceties. I can see how psychologically they may feel Americans are sometimes rude—and vice versa.

But the French have a secret. Many of them actually do speak passable English. If an American asks a Parisian politely if they speak English, most Parisians will answer *"un peu"* (a little). Then they'll begin speaking English to you—and feel relieved since you now know they're also shy about speaking a foreign tongue. If you can mingle in a little French as you converse, French people seem to really open up—in my experience. If they say "non" to Franglish however, you can always use sign language. But beware of counting on your hand. Start with the thumb in France when you count; don't raise your index finger and middle finger when ordering drinks for two or you're likely to get three glasses.

By and large, the French are slowly accepting English as the language of commerce. Many French parents are even hiring English language tutors and getting special classes for their children so they'll be able to speak English fluently. My fellow author and charming wine bar owner, Olivier Magny (*Stuff Parisians Like*) wrote his amusing tongue-in-cheek *exposé* completely in English (with a few French phrases). Reading it, however, one can hear some linguistic snafus because, of course, English is not his first language. Meeting him in person, however, the 30-something French entrepreneur switches adroitly between French and English. So as a Gen-X Parisian, he's part of the newer breed who're very open to Americans practicing their French to bridge the culture gap. (Check out his wine bar near Les Halles called *Ô Château*. It's trendy but not too expensive, and it's a cool people-watching spot.)

There are resources around Paris to help English speakers with the French language. While trolling around the Left Bank one day (near the Sorbonne where lots of book stores and inexpensive clothing shops are located), I came across *Fusac*, a slick tabloid in English for the multilingual, multicultural marketplace. There are dozens of advertisements for English courses, classes, shops, rentals, jobs, and more. There are other resources, particularly on the Left Bank around the universities.

In the experience of Stephen Clarke, humorist and *France Magazine* columnist, "Most of [the French] laugh at France's so-called Toubon law of 1994—named after former Minister of Culture Jacques Toubon—which banned the use of foreign languages in advertisements and government publications...Lots of French people will spontaneously sing the birthday tune in English— *"eppy burst day to yew."* More of these delicious factoids can be found in Clarke's *Merde* series and his hilarious *1000 Years of Annoying the French.*

Still, there are some key French phrases that may help visitors get along and build rapport. Restaurant personnel expect travelers to greet them using proper etiquette. *"Garçon"* is out and *"Monsieur"* or *"Madame"* is expected. *"Bonjour"* is always welcome—even 24 hours a day. (*"Bonjour"* in this case means hello.

You can substitute *"bonsoir"* if it's after 6:00 p.m., but don't say *"bonne nuit"* unless you're in your jammies and about to jump into bed.)

If you don't greet Parisians with at least some morsel of French, they'll typically think you're a prig. I know of an American couple who traveled to Paris and refused to speak French anywhere they went. This really irked their waiter in a particular Left Bank *café*. He refused to serve them anything until they at least said *"Bonjour."* This may be taking it a bit far, but Parisians have a right to their own unique boundary-setting techniques.

On the other hand, there's the cranky French cabby experience of my friend Parker. She arrived in Paris with a girlfriend from Amsterdam. At the time she was a very slim, very blonde 18-year-old with hair all the way to her waist. She was wearing the quintessential flower child ensemble: batik baby tee, a circle skirt, and a pair of espadrilles. "I was utterly clueless about my appeal or that of my even blonder, taller friend." The pair got off the Amsterdam train and hailed a cab to go to a restaurant near the Louvre that had been recommended. Parker told the driver the name of the restaurant, and the driver suddenly stopped the cab in the middle of the Champs Élysée. He whipped around and grabbed her lower jaw, saying, "No, no, no. Leeeeuh Doe Faaaan." He made her practice saying the name of the restaurant, Le Dauphin, until he was satisfied with her pronunciation. He then turned around and drove on.

Cranky indeed.

I've had a little better luck with my French, I think, in that no one has accosted me physically to improve my accent. I've found it helps immeasurably to use the expressions *"excusez-moi, s'il vous plaît"* ("excuse me") and *"merci"* ("thank you") for even the smallest kindness. Most Parisians will give an American points for trying. In some *cafés*, I've found the servers will even cozy up and chat, practicing their English, letting me practice my French, and sometimes together we'll look up words on Google Translate.

My most effective French phrase is this one: *"Mon français est très mauvais, mais j'essaie de pratiquer."* ("My French is very bad, but I try to practice.") I notice this phrase opens doors magically for me in Paris. Most Parisians realize in an instant that I'm trying to communicate, however badly, in their language. Subsequently many of them open up and take me to their collective French breasts after that.

This is not to say that all my French language encounters have been pleasant. I once ran into an elderly lady at a street market. We were both peering into a huge basket of misshapen mushrooms. She suddenly turned to me and spat out, *"Quel genre de champignons sont-ils?"* I looked back at her, stunned. She seemed to actually think I was a local and knew all about French mushrooms!

Flustered, I replied, *"Je ne comprends pas, je suis une Américaine"* ("I don't understand, I am an American"). She snorted and turned away from me like I was an imbecile. Not so charming, I know. But I could empathize with her. If you were 80 years old and maybe on your only outing for the week, wouldn't you want to get food information when you needed it instead of having to deal with some foreigner who didn't speak your language? (I would love to have sneaked a picture of her since she reminded me of my grandmother—only crabbier. But I was afraid she might hit me over the head with her veal chops.)

Yet it's all part of the experience, *n'est-ce pas?*

On another occasion, I had an interesting encounter with the word "wolf." In America, a wolf is a wolf and a fish is a fish. But in Paris, they have other ideas. I was dining with my husband in an elegant *café*. There was a French couple (in scarves of course) on our left and a German couple (in sturdy shoes) on our right. The menu listed *Loup De Mer* as one of the specialties. The descriptor said it was *la plat principal* (main) course cooked in a white wine sauce with lemon and courgettes. Like any good American with limited French, I whipped out my French dictionary; in black and white I read that *loup* meant "wolf."

When the waiter appeared, I asked him innocently, "Is this dish really made with wolf?" The waiter shrank back, horrified. And on either side of us, the French couple and the German couple (who apparently were eavesdropping) erupted into laughter. After much puzzlement, I finally learned that *Loup de Mer* was indeed named after a wolf, but the dish was made from the "wolf of the sea," sea bass.

Who knew?

Hence I was dropped into the waters of French disdain (and maybe a little German too), but who could stay angry for long? The *Loup de Mer* was superb. And washed down with a little *Chenin Blanc*, followed by a *Grand Marnier soufflé* for dessert, who could stay mad?

I'd highly recommend acquiring a little French if you visit France. Even better, research published in the journal *Neurology* shows that bilingual people may be able to hold Alzheimer's at bay. Learning a new language is good for us! It can delay the onset of dementia by up to four years, according to the study. In addition, children who grow up speaking multiple languages appear to be better at multitasking—and fare better in life as a result.

There are some must-have phrases you might want to consider learning. For example, it's really important to learn the word *sortie* (exit) in case of a fire, when leaving the airport, and when leaving the restroom. Others include:

- *Je voudrais...* (I would like...) This is the polite way to ask for something. You can use it in stores, *cafés*, the *métro*, etc.

- *Parlez-vous Anglais?* (Do you speak English?)

- *Où sont les toilettes?* (Where is the bathroom?)

- *Urgence!* (Emergency!)

- *Au secours! (Help!)*

- *Arrête!* (Stop!)

- *Au Feu!* (Fire!)

- *Attention!* (Watch out!)

- *Un policier* or *gendarme* (police officer)

- *Un pompier* (fireman)

- *Auxillaire medical* (paramedic)

- *Avoir besoin* (to need...)

- *Avoir besoin d'un medicin* (to need a doctor)

Once you get comfortable with some basic French, you can order a book of *métro* tickets (*"Je voudrais un carnet de tickets de métro"*), tell store staff you're "just looking" (*"Je ne fais que regarder, merci"*), or order a larger size in a department store (*"J'ai besoin d'une plus grande taille"*). Other useful phrases include "Can you help me?" (*"Pouvez-vous m'aider?"*) and "Can I try this on?" (*"Puis-je assayer?"*). I notice a big difference in the demeanor of staffers, even if I only speak a few French phrases, then switch back to English. The French know I'm making an effort—and in some cases they see me as very approachable and start peppering me with questions. The two 20-something clerks in Diwali (my favorite scarf shop in Paris) buttonholed me once. They wanted to know the English word for that "thing" English speakers were always talking about where they expected to pay. Apparently, many Anglos hunt around Parisian shops looking for a "cash register." The French call it a *caisse enregistreuse* or *contrôler la sortie de* (check out). (Often, there is no register in a French shop or restaurant; they like to use hand held devices to collect payment.)

Thus the linguistic battle goes on. But trying to broaden your language horizons will go far toward enhancing your enjoyment in Paris. By the way, Google Translate is accessible day or night on your phone or hand held device. And of course, there are other programs and phone apps you can use to keep ahead of the language curve—no matter where you are. Of course, carrying a guide book or old fashioned dictionary still works just fine, too.

In sum, I like to remember the words of Claude Gagnière:

> *Un homme qui parle trois langues est trilingue.*
> *Un homme qui parle deux langues est bilingue.*
> *Un homme qui ne parle qu'une langue est anglais.*
> (A man who speaks three languages is trilingual.
> A man who speaks two languages is bilingual.
> A man who speaks only one language is English.)

Creativity

"He who contemplates the depths of Paris is seized with vertigo. Nothing is more fantastic. Nothing is more tragic. Nothing is more sublime."

—Victor Hugo

*T*he *Thinker* sits watching the roses bloom in the lush gardens of the Rodin Museum in the heart of Paris. Like some *mascotte créatif* (creative mascot) forged by Auguste Rodin, he was fashioned from the same creative fires that fueled the talents of Claude Monet, Salvador Dali, Man Ray, James Joyce, Edith Piaf, Victor Hugo, and Ernest Hemingway, among many others. Like a guardian of genius, *The Thinker* watches and waits for the next magnum opus to be birthed in the *Ville Lumière*—City of Light.

What is it about Paris that nurtures artistry?

When I step off the plane at Charles de Gaulle, I don't feel any special vibe. When I travel along the autoroute through the suburban sprawl pockmarked with graffiti toward Paris proper, I don't feel it. But when I reach the city center, with the Eiffel Tower in view and the great walls of the Louvre towering above the Seine, I sense the magic. When my feet finally hit the ground of the Tuileries or the pavement on Quai d'Orsay, I somehow step into the creative womb of Paris.

The intoxication has begun.

It's hard to describe. But there's some heady cocktail of intoxicated enlightenment, creative sparkle, and raw sweat that impregnates the Paris air. Perhaps it's the opulence that animates it: the breathtaking art, the ancient walls, the smell of French food, the vapor of perfumes, the sounds of French conversation mixed with song. Or perhaps it's in the churning populace laboring along the aged streets, as mundane as the corner crepe man or as coutured as designer Sonia Rykiel striding along Rue Saint-Honoré. Or perhaps it's in the foreigners who bring their hopes and dreams to the mix in the creative stew of Paris, birthing the bold, the bizarre, the beautiful.

More likely, the cultural bounty springs from the vitality of artistic and intellectual thought in Paris. The tolerance for innovation is high in the City of Light. And with collegial surroundings like *cafés*, *bistros*, and *tabacs*, artisans can congregate, swap perspectives, glean ideas, and tap into the collective unconscious that generates innovation. Gallery openings are celebrated—and well attended. Museum collections are visited, talked about, remembered. New venues for expression are embraced as daring forays beyond the cultural envelope. Bold artists are noticed and applauded for their efforts.

Friedrich Nietzsche said, "For art to exist, for any sort of aesthetic activity or perception to exist, a certain physiological precondition is indispensable: intoxication." Paris is ripe with intoxication. It makes it easy to take risks there. To open the psyche. To let the city's cultural beauty and quirkiness seep into a fertile mind for rebirth as creative genius.

I'd suggest many Parisians (and the creative souls who go there) simply prefer to live in the right side of their brains, the creative side. Certainly this is a generalization, but my senses prick up when I'm around the music, the artistry, the fashion, the grand experiments in advertising and design and architecture in Paris. It's a continual feast for the senses as I ogle the fabulous department store window displays, for example, or watch all manner of artisans on the street, painting, performing, and selling their creations.

The right brain is alive and thriving in the people of Paris. Yes, this makes for long lines and plenty of red tape. This makes the machinery of life churn lethargically sometimes. But I think this is because in Paris, life makes way for culture, for expression. Art doesn't get pushed aside for life.

As such, the artisan is respected, even glorified. The artist may not be rich, but he or she is honored, perhaps cherished. Paris is not a good city for making motherboards or engines or plastic food containers. It's a place with a right brain calling. I've even been told that in every French man or woman's garage, there's an easel. He or she expects to paint. To perhaps be the next Renoir or Lautrec or even just a mediocre hobbyist. But he or she will paint nonetheless. The creative urge is not just a legacy in France; it's a way of living.

And why not?

Though the capacity for genius may be resident in French genes, foreigners too can pick up the scent, the ripe molecules seeping into our psyches, erupting in flashes of brilliance through brush, pen, chisel, laptop, song, and even movie lens à la Woody Allen. But what exactly is it that feeds this fertile soil of expressiveness in Paris?

Perhaps it's in the charm of the night-lit monuments. Or the pools of romantic light created by the old-fashioned street lamps. Maybe it's the scent of fresh bread, flowers, and wine. But perhaps it's primarily the imposing relics of a people who so prized their "village" on the Seine that they bred, bled, and died there, with new generations taking up the cause to bring illumination to the world.

It was historian Jules Michelet (1798-1874) who probably first dubbed Paris *"La Lumière du Monde"*—Light of the World. He wrote about the changes that grew out of the French Revolution. Changes that toppled centuries of royal rule and forged a brave, new Paris. The population of Paris more than doubled during his lifetime. By the second half of the 19th century, the city had become the epicenter for creativity and *panache* for all of Europe. Philosophers came for the intellectual freedom. Musicians came for the diversity. Artists came for the light. And writers came for the inspiration.

The rubble of rebellion was slowly cleared by the brilliant architects and ingenious city planners of the new Paris. The revitalization reshaped Paris over the next 100 years, bringing with it broad boulevards, citywide lighting, parks and fountains, and the repurposing of royal structures into venues for government and art. Likewise, the philosophies of Rousseau and the great works of romantic literature from Charles

Baudelaire, François-René de Chateaubriand, and Victor Hugo breathed creative life back into the ancient city.

Hugo, portrayed in this sculpture by Auguste Rodin, emerged as a political activist, poet, novelist, and dramatist who helped shape the future of Paris through his powerful ideas. Before his death in 1885, he witnessed: the rise and fall of two Napoléons; the restoration of Notre Dame following the publication of his novel *The Hunchback of Notre-Dame*; and the Paris Uprising of 1832 that sparked his sweeping paean to the downtrodden of Paris, *Les Misérables*. Hailed as a masterpiece, *Les Misérables* became a clarion call to oppressed people everywhere for generations to come:

> "Do you hear the people sing
> Lost in the valley of the night?
> It is the music of a people
> Who are climbing to the light.
>
> For the wretched of the earth
> There is a flame that never dies.
> Even the darkest night will end
> And the sun will rise."

Just as Hugo hoped, the Belle Époche (Beautiful Era) dawned around the 1870s, bringing peace, prosperity, and ingenuity. Life in Paris was transformed with the advent of the automobile, the airplane, movies, cinematography, the telephone, the gramophone, and the glittering Art Nouveau style that shaped the architecture, fashion, and decor of the age. Toulouse-Lautrec captured the cabaret spirit through his paintings and illustrations. Sarah Bernhardt wowed them in the theaters and on the screen. Louis Pasteur invented the rabies vaccine, while the Curies discovered radium. Proust began to publish. Manet, Monet, Degas, Cézanne,

Van Gogh, Gauguin, Rodin, and others produced magnificent art. The chic department store Galeries Lafayette opened on Boulevard Haussmann, the Eiffel Tower was built, and the Grand Palais (Palace for the Fine Arts), a marvel of steel, stone, and glass, rose to celebrate the turn of the century with the latest in French technology and art. Soon, the Citroën, France's first mass-produced car, began barreling through the streets of Paris. Sadly, the beautiful era ended with the sound of gunfire and cannons as World War I erupted in 1914.

From 1914 to 1918, war waged in Europe; more than 37 million lives were lost. By the time writers, artists, and intellectuals straggled back to Paris after 1918, the city's power to inspire was tempered by the somber mood of a generation who had lost their ideals—but had gained a sense of raw realism. Artists, musicians, writers, and filmmakers were galvanized by new movements like Cubism and Surrealism. Picasso, Cézanne, and Man Ray created startling works. Avant-garde entertainers like Josephine Baker, Louis Armstrong, and Edith Piaf packed the cabarets. Daring new fashion appeared on the streets by Elsa Schiaparelli and Coco Chanel. French literature blossomed into a new openness with the titillating works of Jean Cocteau and Colette. Expats like Henry Miller, Samuel Beckett, F. Scott Fitzgerald, and Ernest Hemingway were drawn into the bubbling cauldron of Paris creativity. And Gertrude Stein, muse and bon vivant, regularly stirred the pot.

"A writer should write with his eyes and a painter paint with his ears," Stein explained to the anointed few who came to her Saturday night salons at her home on the Left Bank. These *soirées* were famous for their guidance, inspiration, and sometimes castigation from Stein as the arbiter of taste. Starving artists mixed with acknowledged greats in the milieu of bubbling creativity. The art of Cézanne, Delacroix, Matisse, and Picasso found places on Stein's elegant walls. Often the artists themselves turned up for an *absinthe* or *café crème.*

"America is my country and Paris is my hometown," Gertrude Stein explained. But she delivered an even deeper message. "All of you young people who served in the war...you are all a lost generation," she proclaimed. Ezra Pound, Sinclair Lewis, James Joyce, and Thornton Wilder found inspiration at the Stein Salon along with Hemingway and Fitzgerald, among others. The lost ones explored their post-war angst in such works as Hemingway's *The Sun Also Rises* and *For Whom the Bell Tolls* and Fitzgerald's *The Great Gatsby.*

Around the same time, expat Sylvia Beach took a $3,000 inheritance from her mother and opened Shakespeare and Company, an English-speaking bookstore and lending library on the Left Bank. It quickly became a gathering place for budding writers like Hemingway and Pound, and often also provided the starving artists with a place to sleep and something hot to eat. Shakespeare and Company even published *Ulysses* in 1922 when James Joyce could find no other publisher. Beach helped keep Hemingway nourished and focused. He writes vividly of his Paris life in *A Moveable Feast*, recounting his days of pain and glory. (See the sign of one of his Parisian flats.)

In 1940, however, war came again to France once more when Hitler invaded. The Third Reich took over Paris. The Ritz Hotel was a favorite domicile. Culture, as well as couture, basically went underground. Great works were confiscated or destroyed. Fine wines were hidden from the Germans, but Coco Chanel seems to have thrived by falling in love with a German officer (and living at the Ritz). After five long years, the truce was finally signed. World War II was over. With the Third Reich's capitulation, Paris emerged from years of occupation, and the fires of creation bubbled yet again. (Hemingway personally liberated the bar at the Ritz after the Germans finally left Paris. Ostensibly as a war correspondent, he commandeered a jeep, raced down the Champs-Élysée, zipped across the Place de la Concorde, and skidded to a stop at the Place Vendôme in front of the Ritz. He hopped out and strode into the bar, beating the Allied army to the punch. He immediately ordered champagne for himself and his "irregulars"—everyone who'd been in the jeep with him.)

Simone de Beauvoir and Jean-Paul Sartre laid the ground for liberation and new thought in the post-war period. Le Defense was built to house the new face of French business, and the inside-out Pompidou Centre was constructed to hold the contemporary art of the day. Coco Chanel eventually rose again, bringing back her famous suits and jewelry. And competition from Christian Dior, Cristóbal Balenciaga, and Robert Piguet made Paris the capital of the fashion world. Sartre, Beckett, and Allen Ginsberg launched the sounds of the 1960s beat generation and existentialism. Sartre's play *Huis-clos* (*No Exit*) illustrated the prevailing attitude of the day, particularly his memorable line: "*L'enfer, c'est les autres.*" ("Hell is other people.") But Picasso, perhaps more upbeat than the rest, continued to paint with gusto. "The purpose of art is washing the dust of daily life off our souls." And dust they did.

Today's Paris has one distinctive quality that perhaps makes it unique in the creative world. *All* of these periods of robust expression are accessible to a simple tourist wandering along the avenues of the City of Light. Nowhere else on the planet can you see the Musée d'Orsay's Belle Époque Watch Tower with Eiffel's 1887 tower shimmering behind it, and, as you turn around, glimpse the royal

Louvre begun in the 12ᵗʰ century, while the modern Rue de Rivoli just behind it is selling the latest 2013 iPhone or platform heels.

For the modern visitor, there are a multitude of opportunities for traveling the inspirational paths of these greats who thrived in Paris. And it's pretty simple in the City of Light. Like some kind of cultural time machine, Paris doesn't whisk you between centuries—you simply step into them when you merely cross the street.

Walking tours are a wonderful way to soak up the culture and perhaps derive some inspiration. Paris Walks is one of my favorite English language walking tour companies that offers guided tours of creative Paris. "The Village of Montmartre Tour" for example takes you along the winding streets up to the Basilica of the Sacré Cœur where you'll pass artist studios where the likes of Renoir and Lautrec painted. The magnificent white church, depicted in so many photos and films, stands as a beacon for *créativité* for generations of artisans who nurtured their talents in its shadows. I can feel the inspiration seeping into my bones when I go there; as I look around, smell the aromas, and feel the stones beneath my feet, I sense the fires warming my psyche from the ground up.

Outside and on the hillsides behind Sacré Cœur, you can see the tiny remnants of one of the first vineyards in Paris—when Montmartre was still considered the countryside. This is the ancient Clos Montmartre Vineyard, near Renoir's house. It's just across the street from Lapin Agile Cabaret where wildly famous  artists like Picasso and Modigliani used to hang out, sometimes offering up their artwork in exchange for food. And up the street, you can stand hip to hip with 21ˢᵗ century artists (pictured) who are birthing their modern masterpieces on the very pavements where Maurice Ultrillo and Van Gough might have painted.

Across the Seine on the Left Bank, Paris Walks offers "Hemingway's Paris." The tour meanders through the neighborhoods where the writer lived, worked, shopped, and drank at various locales around the Mouffetard market street and the historic church of St. Etienne-du-Mont. The streets around Place de la Contrescarpe look mostly the same as when Hemingway wrote about them in *A Moveable Feast.* He lived at 74 Rue Cardinal Lemoine—down the street from James Joyce at 71.

In *Midnight in Paris*, Woody Allen has his main character, Gil, sitting on the steps of St. Etienne-du-Mont church when the vintage Peugeot arrives to take him off to meet Hemingway and Fitzgerald at one of Gertrude Stein's *soirées*. You'll also walk by abodes of Orwell and Balzac.

Paris Insight offers the "Les Misérables Tour," highlighting Victor Hugo's Paris and the district of Le Marais where the book is set. Some say the ghosts of Cosette, Marius, and Jean Valjean still haunt the streets. Or you can just wander with no agenda.

You might spy the likes of my fellow creative Marie Thérèse Berger, an exquisite painter now working in Paris. Or you might see author David Sedaris (*Me Talk Pretty One Day*) who frequents the City of Light. You may glimpse pastry chef, author, and bon vivant David Lebovitz (*The Sweet Life in Paris*) who's busy today baking, writing mouthwatering books, and blogging about his quirky experiences in the City of Light. If you frequent the Marais, you may even run into the delightful David Downie, guide, travel expert, and author of *Paris, Paris: Journey into the City of Light*. Downie regularly walks the streets of Paris. On his arm may be his talented wife, Alison Harris, the acclaimed photographer.

On the Left Bank, along the noisy Boulevard Saint-Germain, are the *cafés* Deux Magots, Café de Flore, and the Brasserie Lipp where Faulkner, Camus, Cocteau, Fitzgerald, Breton, and many others congregated to swap ideas (and guzzle plenty of house wine). Stroll down Rue du Bac on your way to big department store Le Bon Marché and you may pass local author, Elaine Sciolino. Sciolino's recent book, *La Seduction,* explores the seductive charms of the French. Stroll east to the Luxembourg Gardens where Zelda and F. Scott Fitzgerald lived nearby or meander further to Rue de Fleurus where Gertrude Stein and Alice B. Toklas had their salon at No. 27. Further south near Montparnasse, you can also find the domiciles of Dalí, Becket, Colette, and Miró.

The Louvre, of course, is the premier location in Paris for viewing collections, old and new. Initially, the massive Louvre palace was the seat of the French monarchy (when they were not languishing at Versailles, hunting game in the Loire Valley, or contemplating the guillotine from the *Conciergerie*). After the French Revolution, the structure was converted into a public institution to safeguard the nation's cultural heritage. It currently houses 380,000 works spanning 6,000 years of art history. Today, it's the most visited museum in the world; in 2010 alone, a staggering 8.5 million visitors perused the priceless art. The Louvre displays such classics as the *Venus de Milo,* Leonardo da Vinci's *La Joconde* (the Mona Lisa), and *Winged Victory*.

The Louvre has even gone high tech. Now not only can you view the nearly 15 acres of masterpieces in the flesh, Louvre-provided Nintendo 3DS handheld video consoles can also show you many of the pieces in 3D—and rotate them for your viewing pleasure. The devices provide detail about the fabulous artwork and help visitors navigate the maze of galleries. The museum also sells smartphone and tablet apps, including mobile versions of the 3DS audio tours. Though I've visited the Louvre five times, I've yet to see it all; my feet give out long before my appreciation does. I often end up at one of the *cafés* strategically situated in the cavernous wings, nursing a large cup of *chocolat* while I gather strength for the next exhibit. Sometimes the apps can fill the gap when your feet can't!

If you get bored with the Louvre, you can try one of the more than 152 other museums in Paris, including the Centre Pompidou and the Musée d'Orsay. And you can gain inspiration for your own projects by watching live artists at work like the one shown. For modernists, there's today's avant-garde scene. Street artists covered in gold or silver mime characters for visitors from every country on the planet. And costumed crusaders, graffitists, street musicians, and what I call "posers" who'll pose for pictures with tourists, fill the streets providing a rich climate of novelty.

Contemporary street art also thrives in Paris—one of the signs of the still-revolutionary spirit there. Mosaic aliens like this one in Montmartre can be found all over Paris, for example. This cult artistry is revitalizing the walls of Paris—with or without the city's consent.

(As a quirky note, aliens are very welcome in France. With tongue-in-cheek innovation, there's even a UFO landing pad in a small town called Arès about 50 kilometers west of Bordeaux. The "UFOport" was installed after France received complaints that the country had no UFO welcome stations for extraterrestrials. As a result, the mayor commissioned the triangular port to be built—and even declared that alien visitors who landed would be exempt from any airport taxes. The plaque at the site reads: "Reserved for voyagers of the universe." As far as I know, there are no alien landing pads in Paris—but I do occasionally see a few out-of-this-world creatures deplaning at Charles de Gaulle.)

Back in Paris, there's creative art in all kinds of places: *on* the walls as pictured and emerging *from* walls as shown.

Paris's aesthetic soul continues to whisper to the artistic heart. Wherever you are in Paris, whatever your interests, your abilities, or your background, the city can ignite your creative spirit. And, in the words of Ernest Hemingway:

"If you are lucky enough to have lived in Paris as a young man, then wherever you go for the rest of your life, it stays with you, for Paris is a moveable feast."

Taste

à table !

Expo

du repas gastronomique en Val de Loire

L'ESPACE D'EXPOSIT
DU LOIR-ET-CHER

"The destiny of nations depends [on] how they feed themselves."

—J.A. Brillat-Savarin, *The Physiology of Taste*

For many of us the phrase "French cuisine" taps a deep memory of irresistible tastes, mouthwatering images, and savory aromas. Succulent *chateaubriand* sizzling next to young asparagus in a tarragon cream sauce. Bubbling *bouillabaisse* brimming with bounty from the sea. Crunchy French bread slathered with ripe *Brie*. Chocolate-laced *mille-feuille* oozing vanilla custard.

Perhaps like many, I can forgive the French anything when *cuisine française* hits my tongue. Who could argue with the creators of such superb food? When we dine in France, we enjoy the largesse of generations who have nuanced the national cuisine to the gastronomical marvel it is today. But that standard can be exacting. Case in point: In 1671, Vatel, the head chef of the Prince de Condé, killed himself with his own sword. Why? The seafood had not arrived in time for a dinner the prince was giving for King Louis XIV.

The modern French chef may feel as mortally wounded if he loses a Michelin star—that coveted barometer of culinary supremacy—but most *cuisiniers* find other ways to dispatch their pain. (If I know anything about French chefs, they probably drown their sorrows in a bottle or two of Grand Cru, then they get back to cooking.)

The French have not only harvested the delicacies of their land, sea, and hillsides, they've codified the tastes, aromas, and preparation of food as well. Cuisine is a science in France. But it also evolves as a highly esteemed art. Many of today's most honored French *artistes* shape their masterpieces not in stone and pigment, but in food and nectar from the grape.

Jean Anthelme Brillat-Savarin, a 19th century French lawyer and gastronome, first popularized the concept of the gastronomical essay. Later he compiled his detailed analysis of the smells, tastes, and pleasures of the French table in his book, *The Physiology of Taste*. This lengthy work is still in print—and assiduously studied—today. Brillat-Savarin wrote, "Tell me what you eat, and I will tell you what you are." Extrapolation: If you're not eating French cuisine, you're eating dross.

How did this fine food come to be?

Centuries ago, French peasants thrived on hearty meals of local vegetables, rabbit, and fish concocted to fill big stomachs on a small-Franc budget. In the grand chateaux up the hill, however, the royals supped on regal meals of shellfish bisque, deep-sea oysters, wild boar, and gold-leaf chocolates washed down with *Dom Pérignon*.

Over the years, the hardiness of French peasant food slowly blended with the royal cuisine, especially after the royals fell and Napoléon had to feed an army of Frenchmen with big appetites. "An army," he proclaimed, "marches on its stomach." One of his minions even invented canned food!

But it took Auguste Escoffier, the "king of chefs," to catalogue the disparate French methods and form a coherent approach to producing fine food. *Haute Cuisine* was born. His 1920 masterwork, *Le Guide Culinaire,* remains the culinary Bible to chefs the world over.

And then came Julia. After World War II, food-loving American Julia Child and her adorable husband Paul, came to live in Paris. She unwittingly stumbled on her life's work when she dined one night in Rouen on an unforgettable meal of oysters, *sole meunière,* and fine wine. Her revelation: If she loved to eat the cuisine so much, why not learn to cook it? Voilà!

After a few Le Cordon Bleu courses and lots of hard work, she emerged as a passable French chef. Soon she was approached by Louisette Bertholle and Simone Beck, who needed help. The pair was struggling to write a French recipe book in English. The goal: to bring French cooking to English speakers. When Child agreed to collaborate on the project, a culinary institution was born.

With the publication of *Mastering the Art of French Cooking* in 1961, America embraced French cuisine with gusto. Child became a sensation. Her books, her life story, and her memorable cooking shows made America realize that the refined tastes and techniques of France were at last accessible to the average home. And they had the eccentric, funny, exuberant Julia Child as their guide.

Child once wrote: "In France, cooking is a serious art form and a national sport." For Americans, however, it can be daunting. I love eating French cuisine (as long as it's not something resembling mucus in a shell (snails) or organ meat from anything with eyeballs). But cooking the French way is not for the fainthearted.

I once prepared Child's recipe for *Potage Velouté aux Champignons* (mushroom soup). Several labor-intensive hours (and sore feet) later, the family and I finally sat down to enjoy the creamy, mushroom-studded concoction imbued with cream and butter. It was heavenly. We enjoyed every drop. Nevertheless, I would keel over if I had to do that every day. Even the few cooking classes I've taken in France were frankly exhausting, though enlightening.

Nevertheless, I do admire Child's approach to being prepared. She advised, "I think every woman should have a blowtorch." And for new and seasoned chefs, Child had some remarkable pearls of wisdom: "The best way to execute French cooking is to get good and loaded and whack the hell out of a chicken. Bon appétit." (I too find French cooking much more fulfilling with a glass of wine next to the cutting board. But I can only have one glass. Any more and I have a tendency to take disastrous short cuts or need a nap before I finish the meal.)

For the great chefs of France, however, *le culinaire* is a mighty calling. The standards are rigorous, and the training is inordinately demanding. Earning a Michelin star for culinary excellence is the prime objective of most French chefs. Getting or losing one can make or break a chef's reputation.

Food is simply serious business in France.

In the finer Parisian establishments, dining is formal. Decorum is keenly observed. Often, the ambiance of a high-end Parisian restaurant matches the exquisite dishes, food presentation, and fine wines that are offered with great solemnity. The high-end restaurants particularly earn their stars—and justify their prices—since they labor to maintain their rankings. The more casual eateries like *bistros*, *brasseries*, and *cafés* are an alternative. They also offer wonderful French food but at more reasonable prices, in a more relaxed setting.

When I first visited Paris, I was confused by all the eatery designations. To this day, some of the boundaries blur for me. But here's a brief recap. *Le Bistro* is considered a bar or *café*. It provides medium-priced, standard French food and drinks at roughly 15-30 euros per person. The atmosphere is bustling. The *décor* is often quaint or historical with menus written on blackboards. The food is frequently served on smallish round tables. As shown in this photo, hyper-efficient servers typically dressed in black slacks and big white aprons do the service. *Cafés* are included in this category.

The French word *Brasserie* origi-
nally meant "brewery." *Brasserie* soon
became the designation for the large,
busy Parisian restaurants that are
open late and don't require a reservation. The *décor* often has distressed
menus, tiles floors, and red booths.
The menus are extensive; three course
meals are the norm. Specialties like
steak frites, *escargot*, soups, stews, and
seafood trays are often served. But *plat du jour* (plate of the day) is a common meal. Prices are higher than *bistros* and run roughly 30-70 euros per person. An example is *Le Train Bleu Brasserie*, featured in many guidebooks.

Les Restaurants are the ultimate in French gastronomy. The best French chefs like Alain Ducasse, Bernard Loiseau, and Guy Savoy helm fabulous restaurants where the latest evolution of French cuisine is served. Many top Paris restaurant lists are available, but some I can mention are Le Grand Véfour, Guy Savoy, La Tour d'Argent, Taillevent, Le Cinq (Four Season Hotel George V), and the Jules

Verne (Eiffel Tower). If you're not prepared to lay down the cost of a mortgage payment for your tab, avoid these places. If money is not a concern, reserve a table and enjoy.

I love the dining variety in Paris. There's great French food for any budget. Even the wine is cheap if you go for the house wine; sometimes you can get a decent glass for as little as three or four euros. Some of my favorite places are the more comfortable *cafés* and *brasseries* like Café de la Paix, Brasserie ma Bourgogne, Le Balzar, Le Fontaine de Mars, and Au Bon Accueil.

Paris visitors often like to see the legendary *cafés*. Many guidebooks tout the Left Bank's Café de Flor and Les Deux Magots depicted in the photo. These eateries served Hemingway, Sartre, Picasso, and scores of others from the "lost generation." And the *cafés* charge you for the privilege of smelling the air these greats once breathed. Unfortunately, both have become overcrowded tour bus magnets with bland food, in my opinion. (I once had a *croque-monsieur* at Les Deux Magots that tasted like Velveeta cheese on cardboard.)

There are small gems, however, like Chez l'Ami Jean near the Eiffel Tower, where you eat family style or Le Timbre ("the Postage Stamp") where you can dine in one of the world's teeniest restaurants on some of the best-rated cuisine in Paris for a shockingly affordable price. (And rub elbows with the local French who will be less than a foot away!)

President Obama and his wife Michelle dined at La Fontaine de Mars (pictured) when they were in Paris a couple of years ago. It's not terribly expensive, it's easy to get to, and it has terrific food. Hanging on the wall is a plaque (pictured) telling diners that Obama enjoyed one of the restaurant's specialties from Southwest France called tarbais (beans), which are often served in *cassoulet*. *Cassoulet* is the chicken and bean casserole baked for hours in a wine reduction sauce. It's superb.

Of the top Paris restaurants, I've only dined at a handful of them. La Tour d'Argent is one of the oldest (and most expensive) restaurants in Paris. My husband and I had an eventful experience there one November. First, a bit of background. La Tour d'Argent hails from the 16th century when it served as an inn for aristocrats. (Louis XIV and the French court dined there.) Though the original structure was burned down during the French Revolution, it was rebuilt after 1870. It's been serving grand cuisine and fine wine ever since.

La Tour d'Argent also played a daring role in World War II. The Demarcation Line was drawn in France, and the Germans were about to seize Paris in 1940. Terrified for the establishment's treasure trove of fine wine, the owner's son and heir apparent, Claude Terrail, hatched a plan. On a six-day pass from his air force duties, Terrail dashed to Paris. There, he and a trusted employee Gaston Masson, took heroic steps. They hastily built a false wall at the back of the massive wine cellar. There, they hid thousands of bottles of the finest French wines so the German High Command couldn't get at them. Men, women, and children all helped. Even cobwebs and spiders were gathered to adorn the new wall; it had to look antique.

When the Germans descended on Paris, Field Marshal Hermann Goring immediately dispatched an emissary to La Tour d'Argent. His purpose: to confiscate the most famous of its wines, the grand cru vintages from 1867. Upon arrival, the emissary was told by restaurant staff that the fine wines, *malheureusement* (regrettably), had all been drunk.

Of course the Germans suspected subterfuge. Though Goring's soldiers searched and searched, the incomparable wines were never found. Though the soldiers seized the remaining 80,000 modest bottles, the Germans regularly dined at the restaurant during Hitler's occupation—and reportedly even paid for their meals!

Later, the wall was removed and the fine wines served as the basis for the restaurant's current collection. It now numbers more than 450,000 bottles. The ponderous wine cellar is reportedly guarded around the clock. Its contents are valued at about 25 million euros ($32 million). When the wine list is brought to your table, the sommelier presents a hefty 400-page wine "list" filled with 15,000 wine choices. It resembles a Bible. But it lifts like the Chicago phone book. When we dined there, we ordered a budget bottle. Price: 190 euros ($247).

At today's La Tour d'Argent, much of the magic remains. Using my fractured French in a flowery email, I had begged for a window table for our anniversary dinner. It seemed to do the trick. The French, ever romantic, were happy to oblige. We were seated at one of the bay window tables often featured in the guidebooks. Across the way, we could see the magnificent lights of Notre Dame sparkling in the roiling Seine.

We expected a culinary extravaganza. We were not disappointed. Though diners can also enjoy such delicacies as *Crêpes Belle Époque* and *Pike Dumplings André Terrail,* La Tour d'Argent is renowned for its delectable duck. And not just any duck. The restaurant raises the feathered creatures on its own farms to ensure quality. These ducks even have their own certifications. At the end of a meal, a *dîner de canard* is presented with a special certificate listing the serial number of the bird consumed (see photo). Naturally, we ordered duck. And we were treated like royalty. Course after course arrived, interrupted by delightful *amuse bouche* that cleansed our palates as we awaited the next presentation. Finally, a procession of solemn servers brought in a steaming platter with the ceremonial birds aboard. Wheeling over a mobile cutting board, three of the servers carved, plated, and presented our ducks as only the French can do. Heavenly.

Amusingly, the more we ate, the more the head server hovered around my husband. They began to chat, and we soon drew more attention from the staff. As the final course was eaten and cleared, we learned that our cheerful server was actually a German national. He'd married a French girl and become a French citizen. He admitted he was partial to us because my husband, though native born in England, looked German to him! Hence, he thought all evening that he was serving a countryman! (In France, you never know from whence you may yield some influence.)

La Tour d'Argent has also been the inspirational setting for the movie *Ratatouille.* In *Ratatouille,* a culinary-savvy rat creates food to die for in a kitchen inspired by the restaurant's cookery. Though the real La Tour d'Argent has sadly lost a Michelin star or two in recent years (hopefully nothing to do with cinematic rodents who cook French cuisine), it's still a destination for those who want an unforgettable dining experience. But dress up—and make your reservations well in advance.

Across town, I once dined at another of the grand restaurants, with rather disappointing results. The Jules Verne restaurant sits 125 meters above ground level in the Eiffel Tower. From its gleaming perch, one can see all of Paris (if you get a good table). Reservations must be made months in advance. Once you arrive on site, getting into the Jules Verne is a little like getting into Fort Knox. Diners have to cluster at the Jules Verne elevator at the base of the west leg of the tower. From there, your party is allowed in the elevator only if you're on the "list." When the elevator finally opens to permit the "anointed" to enter, diners are then ported up to restaurant level. When the doors open, you step out into a hushed dining room with panoramic views. To me it felt a bit like entering the space shuttle (not that I've been in the shuttle, but Jules Verne was vaguely encapsulated and looked ready for takeoff.)

For this dining experience, I was with a party of six Americans; unfortunately, we got the "American treatment." We weren't seated at one of the grand-view windows. Instead, we sat at a banquet-sized table near the rear of the establishment. Despite the disappointing seating, the service was still professional and the food was delicious. Each of the five courses, which included pan-seared beef *tournedos*, *souffléd* potatoes, and *blanquette de veau* (veal), was presented by a small army of servers who reverently placed the delicacies before us. The desserts were particularly appealing. (Note the Armagnac being poured into the poached apple nesting in white chocolate sauce in this photo.) I enjoyed the meal in general, but I was underwhelmed by the treatment.

On the other hand, I once found myself strangely on the power end of a Parisian dining adventure. At Le Violon d'Ingres, the notable Christian Constant venue, I ran into a French desire-to-please I hadn't encountered before. With reservations again made months in advance, my companion and I were seated. Then, after an aperitif and amuse-bouche, we ordered a beautiful four-course meal. Soon, our *salades césar* appeared. After a few bites, I stopped eating and fiddled with my fork as my companion wolfed down his salad. I did feel the lettuce was a bit over-dressed, but in reality I suddenly felt bilious. I'd been noshing on French goodies all day—and I'd had a huge lunch; now, at 8:00 in the evening, I felt full. The more I pushed my salad around my plate, however, the more the server hovered. From a Parisian perspective, he interpreted my reluctance to mean that I hated the meal.

We were suddenly the most discerning diners in the room. I noticed two more servers join the first. The three began watching me with what I interpreted as alarm. When I finally signaled the salad to be removed, the main server picked up the plate and studied my face with concern.

As the next courses arrived, we had the server's full attention. If I needed water, he was there instantly. If I dropped my napkin, he was at my elbow with another. Though my fish was sublime, I still couldn't eat very much. The server asked me twice (in English and in French) if my meal met with approval. He offered to bring me something else or another item. When I demurred, he stepped back slightly out of sight this time, but I could see him wringing his hands and mumbling.

Pretty soon, he was urging me to eat outright. (Perhaps he thought I had an eating disorder.) Instantly, he sensed my annoyance.

I really wasn't angry with him. It was that we'd hit a major cultural impasse regarding food. In Paris, French diners eat every morsel. (The French couple to our left, for example, ate *everything* on their plates. They even asked for extra bread so they could sop up every bit of the French sauces. I noticed them glance over to our full plates with raised eyebrows.)

But for stuffed Americans, there's simply no doggy bag option in France. In the U.S., I would have simply asked for a to-go container, and the server wouldn't have cared whether I ate the meal or not. But in Paris, picking at your expensive food is simply *not done*. What's more, to send back more than half of your plate translates to "this food is *merde*." I felt sorry for the poor man and gamely ate a few morsels. (Does this make me food co-dependent? Perhaps.) He beamed every time I managed another bite.

When it finally came time for dessert, my companion and I ordered one to share. But the server brought two anyway— "compliments of the management." He looked relieved when we cleaned the dessert plate. But in the way of *haute cuisine*, we were then served *another* dessert (four bon bons) as an after-dessert accompaniment with our coffee. Whew! (This is not the first time I've been served four or five desserts over the course of a French meal.)

When I finally waddled out of Le Violon d'Ingres, several staff members asked me if the meal pleased me. When I concurred, they still looked a bit doubtful. As I turned to lumber down the street to my hotel, I think I felt two of them watching me like rejected lovers. Perhaps a projection on my part? Perhaps not.

And then there's cheese and wine: the milk-based foodstuff and liquid of the gods that makes France a gourmet's mecca. Dozens of shops in Paris are devoted solely to cheese or wine products. The proprietors are usually helpful in locating just the right product for each buyer. But cheese is complicated. France produces more than 400 varieties. (Only a tiny fraction of them are shown in the photo.) Many are deliciously rich and practically run off your plate. Some are exotically stinky. Step into a *fromagerie* in any area of France, and your nose will immediately tell you which is which.

I once entered a Paris cheese shop, and as I scanned the creamy mounds in the massive glass case, my eyes spied a crumbling wheel of blue-veined *fromage*. I requested *une tranche* (a slice). The proprietor studied me for a moment and suddenly wagged his finger gently at me saying, "No Madame, you do not want that cheese. *Mauvaise odeur* (bad smell)." Then he held his nose. I laughed. He laughed. Then I pointed to the milder *Comté*. He gladly sliced off a tiny taste and all was well.

Ergo, when it comes to French cheese, Dorothy, you're not in Wisconsin any more. The ripened *Brie* many of us Americans know and love is quite different in France. Some versions will knock your socks off. *Roquefort*, that wonderful raw sheep's milk cheese with blue mold that's matured in caves in Southern France, will not only put your nose on high alert, it can be iffy nourishment since the non-pasteurization can result in listeria infection. (But with a cool glass of *Châteauneuf-du-Pape* to wash it down, who cares?)

Brie de Meaux is not the pasteurized milk *Brie* we buy in the dairy case at Vons. This is a raw cow's milk cheese that's covered in a thick, white mold meant to be consumed, not scraped away—despite the fact that it looks like spackle. My sister once brought back a big slab of the stuff on an American Airlines flight from Paris. It stunk up the cabin for 11 hours; no one could figure out from whence the horrific smell came. When she deplaned, she and the other passengers finally realized the culprit was her carryon bag. The other passengers scooted down the jetway away from her. My sister ditched the foul-smelling stuff at the first trashcan.

Epoisses, a favorite cheese of Napoléon, is actually banned from public transportation vehicles all over France. Why? Because of its harrowing smell. Even the French have trouble eating this one. Then there's *Camembert de Normandie*. This famous French cheese smells a little like something harvested from one of Lafayette's boots. It's rich in ammonia, sodium chloride, and succinic acid. Smells like it too. I can enjoy Camembert in America; in France I try to sit across the street from it.

The French love their cheese, nevertheless. Centuries ago Brillat-Savarin wrote: "A dessert without cheese is like a beautiful woman with only one eye." I'm not sure I'd go that far, but I do enjoy a little mild, runny cheese with a good port. Today Brillat-Savarin lends his name to one of the most delicately scented mounds of cheesy deliciousness created in France—and brought to a supermarket near you. Americans can now buy a 3-inch sliver of this at Whole Foods market for about $16. Very pricey. Fabulously rich. Not too smelly.

But too much cheese is too much cheese. I once took a cooking course with a delightful French chef (pictured) who whipped out a laminated map of France. He placed a large platter of cheeses next to it. Over the next hour, he cut off little slices of each variety of cheese for all of us to taste, then asked us to guess which region of France produced it. After we guessed (usually wrongly), he'd smack the cheese down on the appropriate area and tell us the history of its production. In general, I like cheese, but after 20 or so of these nibble-and-guess lecturettes, my stomach hit a lactose intolerance wall. I couldn't eat cheese for a week.

But for the French, cheese is a part of every day eating. The smellier the better.

Then there's wine.

France produces about eight billion bottles a year—the most in the world after Italy. French law (yes, *law*) divides wine into four categories. These important distinctions must be shown on the label. There are dozens of varieties that are laboriously harvested and lovingly bottled all over France. Wine growing regions include Bordeaux, Burgundy, Champagne, Languedoc-Roussillon, Loire, Provence, and Normandy, to name a few.

I'm no expert in wine. And in better French eating establishments the most revered person in the place will be the *sommelier* who will direct diners to just the right French wine(s). When beckoned, this wine expert will saunter over to your table and lean in to assess your wine intelligence and your needs. He or she will endeavor to be polite; unless you have a certification in wine, however, you'll most likely feel intimidated. If you can get past the first blush of condescension, you'll find that your French sommelier can be your best friend in a Paris restaurant. Note for Americans: stand your ground. You don't have to buy a mega-expensive bottle of Lafite-Rothschild unless you really want to. After all, you're paying.

Or you can simply shop in the wine stores or street markets and take home some lovely but inexpensive wines to your domicile. Yes, I mean inexpensive. My husband and I once stood, mouths agape, in front of a wine wall in a grocery store in Paris. There were bottles and bottles of fabulous wines for under $7. We bought a few (okay, several). All were wonderful. True story.

But for those who really want to understand all manner of French wine (or other wines for that matter) look no further than *The Wine Bible* by Karen MacNeil. She's distilled wine down to the basic facts—and you can enjoy a glass of chilled *Sancerre* while you digest it.

In summary, can there be any more important experience in France than to sample the food and nectar of kings—and French peasants? In the words of the French, *"Mangez bien, riez souvent, aimez beaucoup."* ("Eat well, laugh often, love abundantly.")

Indulgence

"I feel the end approaching. Quick, bring me my dessert, coffee, and liqueur."

—J.A. Brillat-Savarin's great aunt Pierette

The art of baking bread, creating pastries, and crafting gourmet chocolates has reached the pinnacle of culinary sophistication in France. But it all starts with bread as the staple of French food.

Bread is practically a religion in France. That is, it's carefully regulated. It's created with extreme care. And it's part of a bread indulgence that extends to the daily life of every single French person. Parisians buy their daily bread at the local *boulangerie* or bakery. Most *boulangeries* feature many types of bread made or delivered daily to maximize freshness. The *pâtisserie* or pastry shop may also offer breads, but its focus is mainly on sumptuous pastries, cakes, and other desserts. Many French bakeries are now offering pastries as well, so the line between the two often blurs.

Not surprisingly, France has more bakers per capita than any other country. And the *baguette* is revered as not only the staff of life in France, but practically as a member of the family. *Baguettes* are cared for like a precious commodity in bakeries, often out of reach of patrons, but available for sale the moment they come out of the oven. When they're purchased, the long-limbed crusty goodness is placed in a handy sleeve for the walk home. If it's not consumed right away at home, it's sometimes wrapped in a tea towel to preserve freshness and flavor. Bakeries typically produce *baguettes* throughout the day so that people can buy bread for almost any meal. And they need to. French local law bans the use of fat in bread, which is vital to the long-life process. And there are no preservatives. If not eaten within a day, these icons of French cuisine will be as inedible as plaster.

The most famous bread in France is, of course, the long *baguette* or "French stick." But there are several kinds of *baguettes*: an ordinary half-pound *baguette* with a crisp brown crust; the molded *baguette* (*baguette moulée*) manufactured in an industrial oven, with a lattice pattern underneath; and a floured *baguette* (*baguette farinée*), with a pale crust.

And there are other wonderful French breads including the *couronne* (ring bread), the *flute* (large *baguette*), the *batard* (normal loaf), and the *ficelle* (long, very thick loaf). *Pain de campagne* is thick-crusted country bread, which often has whole wheat or rye flour blended in to help the bread stay fresh. And of course there are whole meal breads, sourdough breads, and the most wonderful of sweet breads, the heavenly *brioche* with the little rounded top popping up. As in most American bakeries, the French also bake up spiced bread with nuts, olives, bacon, cheese, and a variety of other flavorful additives.

The *croissant*, that buttery *viennoiserie* bread roll shaped in the form of a crescent, is another French delicacy that's been around since the Middle Ages. The dough is cut with butter, then rolled and folded several times to create a puff pastry. It's little known, but the modern croissant has morphed into a fast food explicitly in answer to America's wealth of foods to go. More than 40% of the croissant dough in France is fast frozen. Thus, it can be thawed and popped in an oven by unskilled employees. It remains the core of the classic continental breakfast.

In May of 1998, the French government passed a law stating that only bakers who made their dough and baked their bread at the premises could have the designation *artisans boulangers* (bakers). If the sign outside the shop doesn't say this, the shop is a *depot de pain* where bread is deposited (delivered) only, but not made fresh on the premises.

The Grand Prix de la Meilleure Baguette de Paris is the grand *baguette* bake-off where Parisian bakeries vie for the grand prize with their best creations. They're judged on baking technique, taste, crumb density, and *baguette* appearance. In 2012, the prize was won by Sébastien Mauvieux at Boulangerie Mauvieux in the 18th arrondissement. (The 18th arrondissement has produced the last three year's winners, so there must be something in the air—or water—there.) The winner gets a cash prize and a 12-month contract to supply bread to the Élysée Palace, the presidential residence (similar to the White House).

Éric Kayser is the rock star of bread in Paris. With 18 locations throughout the city, you can easily pass by a black and orange Eric Kayser store (and many have *cafés* attached). You'll start salivating as soon as your nose detects the wonderful loaves, baguettes, and rolls of sourdough that line the bountiful shelves.

A famous *boulangerie artisanale* is Poilâne (pictured), known for its sublime sourdough loaves with the distinctive P on every loaf. Baker Lionel Poilâne founded it in 1932. He was determined to bake a sourdough loaf, which would last up to a week and have a distinctive taste to rival the delectability of the *baguette*. His recipe? Stone-ground flour, sea salt from Guérande, pure water, and a rising agent—all mixed into distinctive round loaves baked in wood-fired ovens. It's now so popular that people have it shipped all over the world to their homes for a mere 22 euros a loaf (plus shipping). The website has an adorable "shop" where you can drop the various breads and other products into your "basket." Fans leave adoring poetry on the website, and even Salvador Dali raved about it in 1977: *"Poilâne, c'est le Français vivant que je préfère!"* ("Poilâne, the French living I prefer!")

What's the secret of French bread making?

Even Julia Child had failure after frustrating failure until she finally consulted with Professor Calvel of L'Ecole Française de Meunerie in Paris. He shared the secrets: fine French flour, a very hot oven, and intermittent mists of moisture during the baking process. (The moisture is the magic key to forming a crusty crust around the chewy bread inside.) Child finally had her authentic French loaf. "Like the sun in all its glory suddenly breaking through the shades of gloom," she wrote after finally enjoying her own authentic, handmade French bread.

And now the venerable baguette has even morphed into fast food. It used to be that Paris, like other French cities, abhorred the idea of food eaten on the run. But I often see young men and women striding along the streets of Paris munching on a fresh baguette filled with meat or cheese, lettuce, and tomatoes. *Voilà!* Exquisite food to go—in the City of Light.

After bread comes one of the most important food indulgences in France: sweets. Parisian *pâtisseries* have been around since the 19th century, producing intricately crafted cakes, cookies, custards, pastries, and chocolates in an ever-expanding assortment of exquisite flavors like the display pictured.

Just to name a few, there are: *gâteaux* (cakes) with chocolate, cream, fruit, or nuts (or all four); *petits fours* made from *génoise* cake and frosted with fondant; puff pastries like the fabulous Napoléon (*mille-feuille*) stuffed with *crème anglaise* (custard), *frangipane* (almond cream), or *crème au beurre* (butter cream frosting); *bavarois*, or molded cold desserts of whipped cream, fruit puree, meringue, chocolate, or liquor, set with gelatin and cream; *crêpes* filled with cheese, fruit, or cream; *entremets* (flan or pudding); poached desserts like pear or apple in liquor; *compotes* or *mousses* made with egg whites, cream, and perhaps gelatin. And there are *tartes* of all sorts: apple, plum, strawberry, apricot, lemon, and pear; *Viennoiseries* (Vienna-style breads) made from yeasted dough to create *pain au chocolat* (chocolate croissant), *chausson* (turnover), and *brioche* (cake-like rolls); *macarons* (*crème* filled meringue cookie); and *guimauves* (marshmallows, especially chocolate covered ones in the shape of tiny bears called *oursons guimauve* of which more than 400 million are consumed in France every year).

But these fabulous sweets aren't made by mere amateurs. The art of making fine confections is gleaned after years of backbreaking training in pastry techniques, ingredient combining, chocolatry, decoration, design, microbiology, baking, and presentation. In the mesmerizing documentary film, *Kings of Pastry*, D.A. Pennebaker and Chris Hegedus follow a group of world-class pastry chefs as they compete for France's most prestigious craftsman award: *Meilleur Ouvrier de France* (MOF). Winners are allowed to wear the blue, white, and red striped collar on their chef smocks for life. It's the ultimate recognition of excellence in their field. The President of France presents the awards. The film follows four esteemed pastry chefs in the three-day final competition. They must produce a mind-boggling variety of French pastries from small bites to sensational sugar sculptures in the prescribed amount of time before a panel of hypercritical judges. It's a bit like watching the Olympics, but with pastry athletes up to their eyeballs in sugar.

I had the pleasure of taking a cooking lesson from one of the winners of this very difficult contest. Christophe Quantin of the Lycée d'Hôtellerie de Blois, is not only an MOF, he's also a *Chevalier* in the Order of Academic Palms. He patiently showed us amateurs how to put together a *tarte Tatin*, the famous upside-down tart with caramelized apples. The likable Chef Christophe took us

expertly through the process of creating this renowned French dessert from apple preparation to building the crust to final product.

This experience gave me a profound appreciation for the

complexity of these mouthwatering desserts, as well as for the years of toil that go into becoming one of the artisans of France who create them. Bottom line: I'd rather eat them than make them. And there's plenty of opportunity in Paris.

On nearly every other street in the City of Light, you'll find a *boulangerie*, *pâtisserie*, or *chocolaterie* where you can buy these delicious confections. *The Pâtisseries of Paris* by Jamie Cahill with photos by Alison Harris is a delightful resource with full color photos for Paris visitors who want a crash course in French sweets. The book guides you arrondissement by arrondissement to the yummiest places in Paris. Included are pastry shops, tea salons, bakeries, and chocolate boutiques. Here are few of my favorites.

In the tea salons/pastry stores like the Salon de Thé Angelina, Ladurée, and Dalloyau, you'll find flaky pastries, rich cakes, fruit tarts, and all the *macarons* you can eat accompanied by a large variety of tea, hot chocolate, or coffees. (My favorite is *Café Viennois*, which is a single shot of espresso topped with a thick pile of whipped cream.)

Angelina's is known for brewing the best cup of *chocolat chaud* (hot chocolate) in Paris. This classic French tea salon first opened on the Rue de Rivoli near the Louvre in 1903. Austrian confectioner, Antoine Rumpelmayer, established the high-end tearoom and named it for his beloved daughter-in-law. Since then, it's been a favorite of Marcel Proust, Coco Chanel, Audrey Hepburn, and modern celebrities like Britney Spears and Catherine Deneuve. Angelina's promotes itself as a "luxury brand with a prestigious image that symbolizes the 'French Way of Life.'" It's famous for *Mont Blanc* (a cake made with meringue, whipped cream, and chestnut vermicelli), *le chocolat Africain* (served with a pot of rich whipped cream), and a Belle-Époque interior complete with marble-topped tables and gilded ironwork. From what I've seen, the famous regulars are seated along the wall at the entry while the tourists are clumped together in the center tables. They sip their hot chocolate and try to take surreptitious pictures of the more glamorous Parisians. (I once thought I spied Catherine Deneuve sitting alongside the mirrored wall, but decorum kept me from sneaking a picture of her nibbling her tart.)

Ladurée, the renowned Paris tea *salon-pâtisserie* founded in 1862, has taken the lovely *macaron* to new heights. This heavenly cookie is one of France's most beloved sweets. Pierre Hermé is known as the current master of the *macaron*. Hermé trained as a pastry chef in the 1970s, then became head pastry chef of Fauchon, the high-end gastronome boutique, and later of Ladurée. The foodie Catherine de Medici is credited with bringing the *macaron* to France where the first recipe was published in the 17th century. The *macaron* became a staple in the court of Versailles courtesy of the Dalloyau family; Dalloyau offspring now operate the famous Dalloyau *pâtisseries* sprinkled throughout Paris. Pierre Hermé has also branched out with shops, books, signed collections, and a burgeoning retail industry.

Sofia Coppola famously showed her Marie Antoinette in the film of the same name starring Kirsten Dunst devouring *macarons*, provided by an obliging Ladurée (even though it wasn't until the 19th century when the cookies became sandwiched with a filling). The film shows the doomed queen munching her way through platters of colorful *macarons*: pistachio, lemon-lime, strawberry candy, hazelnut, Venezuelan chuao chocolate and blackcurrant, fig and date, apple, orange-ginger, coconut, black sesame, salted prune, and green tea, to name a few. (See this delicious *macaron* tower in Printemps.)

Then there's chocolate.

The French love affair with choc-olate began nearly 400 years ago. Cor-tés first introduced chocolate to Eu-ropeans in 1528 when he returned to Spain from Mexico. He brought back samples of cocoa beans, cultivated by the Aztecs for thousands of years and used in a ceremonial drink known as xocolatl. Intrigued but put off by the bitter flavor of cacao, the Spanish cre-ated their own version of the Aztecs'  traditional chocolate drink by adding milk, sugar, and vanilla. A century later, in 1615, France's King Louis XIII married Anne of Austria, daughter of the Spanish king. The new queen introduced hot chocolate to the French court. Some years later, King Louis XIV's wife, Marie-Thérèse of Austria, became the second French queen known for her love of chocolate. Chocolate rapidly became a necessity in Versailles, and on 28 May 1659, Louis XIV appointed a valet in the queen's household, David Chaillou, to open the very first chocolate shop in Paris.

Chaillou's monopoly on the preparation and sale of chocolate beverages and sweets lasted nearly 30 years before competition ar-rived on the scene. Chocolate really began to take off under King Louis XV, yet it remained very much an exclusive luxury enjoyed by the nobility, the rich, and the famous.

It soon gained a reputation as an aphrodisiac, and 18th century French art and literature were filled with erotic imagery inspired by chocolate. In 1780, Marie Antoinette even had her own private *chocolatier*. Following the French Revolution, chocolate, like many other goods, became accessible to the masses. Today, chocolate making is not only creative cuisine in France, it's conceptual art since many *chocolatiers* have taken to sculpting the delicious stuff. (See the fabulous purse sculpted in chocolate below.)

Parisians take their chocolate very seriously. I once spied a beautiful storefront in the 5th arrondissement, for example. It was white and gold with sparkling glass. Glamorous photos of women's faces adorned the walls. When I entered the shop, I expected jewelry or high-end cosmetics. But then I noticed the steel counters, scales, clipboards, and tiny cases showing dozens of petite products. Once I inhaled, the scent of chocolate wafted over me like a gale of cocoa goodness. This stunning shop was devoted entirely to chocolate!

In Paris, there are many of these *bijou comme chocolateries* (jewel-like chocolate shops) that feature the most delicate and expensive chocolates made in France. The stores are specially fitted with tasting drawers at the back of the display cases. Behind the counters sit elegantly dressed sales staff wearing white gloves. When the customer indicates a certain flavor, the ladies pull back the tasting drawer and place a delicious sample on a tiny porcelain plate for the taster to sample.

These stores feature the wares of the *crème de la crème* of artisanal French chocolate crafting. These *chocolatiers*—from the head chefs to the lowly minions—have made chocolate their life's work. As American blogger and pastry chef David Lebovitz says on his delightful blog dedicated to Paris, these pros don't make chocolates as part-time work or as second jobs. They've made chocolate their focus as a life-long pursuit of gastronomical perfection.

Not surprisingly, there are more chocolate shops in the City of Light than in any other city in the world. (The Paris phone directory lists more than 300.) It's important to note that traditional French dark chocolate is unique in that it's the least sweetened chocolate in the world, with a typical cocoa content ranging from 62% to 86% or more. Because the French use less butter, cream, and sugar in their chocolates, French chocolate is also less fattening. Indeed, much has been written on its health virtues: high-quality dark chocolate (with more than 70% cacao content) is said to protect the cardiovascular system, lower bad cholesterol, and aid digestion, to name but a few of its benefits.

And it all tastes so wonderful too.

French *chocolatiers* are magicians with flavors, essences, and textures. They contrive sensational sweets infused with such delicacies as exotic fruits, spices, licorice, herbs like basil and thyme, and essence of flowers like rose and lilac. These unique flavors are referred to as the *bouquet*. And the secret alchemy of these chocolates, known as *bon bons*, is suspiciously guarded. *Chocolatiers* compete throughout Paris for the most enticing treats—and adoring customers.

Some popular Parisian chocolate shops include La Maison du Chocolat, Michel Cluizel, Patrick Roger, Jacques Genin, Jean-Charles Rochoux, Franck Kestener, and Christian Constant, among others. Christian Constant has two shops in Paris, one close to the Luxembourg Gardens. He's particularly well known for delicacies like raspberry ganaches, chocolates with spicy or herbal notes, or his famous *palet d'or* confected from fresh cream and dark chocolate. Christian Constant also offers a superlative selection of cakes, pastries, and five heavenly varieties of hot chocolate.

Michel Cluizel chocolates have been famous since the mid-20th century, when Cluizel first opened a family-run shop in Normandy. One of the few *chocolatiers* to process their own carefully selected cocoa beans, Michel Cluizel's chocolates are known for their distinct, balanced flavors. Store visitors can enjoy delicious dark or milk bars, each produced from a distinct blend of cocoa beans in Cluizel's *chocolatier*. Whole cocoa beans can also be purchased.

La Maison du Chocolat was opened in 1977 by Robert Linxe, the "*Ganache* Magician." La Maison's chocolates feature not more than 65% cocoa in their confections, thereby eliminating any bitterness. It has several locations in Paris, as well as in New York, London, Hong Kong, and Tokyo. There's also a huge outlet at Charles de Gaulle airport for those who want to take a few kilos home on the plane. (Your nose will lead the way.)

La Maison's "timeless *ganaches*" flavored with Venezuelan coffee beans, caramel, tea, fennel, almond, or vanilla are sold along with truffles, fruited chocolates (infused with lemon, pistachio, and raspberry), *éclairs* (with chocolate, caramel, or café fondant), *macarons*, tarts, and cakes.

But all this scrumptious chocolate comes with a steep price. I once ordered $100 worth of product from the New York La Maison store for delivery in California. The shipping was an additional $25. When the goods finally arrived, I eagerly tore open the box, pulled out the wrapping paper and filler, and sadly found five teeny little boxes barely five by seven inches in circumference. Each box contained a paltry 6-10 pieces of delectable goodness, each piece the size of a small eraser. Big expense. So little satisfaction.

Parisian chocolate is so much better in person. One afternoon, I was wandering around the Right Bank near Place de Madeleine, home of the famous Madeleine Church. I noticed a little byway called Le Village Royal. Stepping onto the artful cobblestones, I suddenly came upon a massive, yawning chocolate hippopotamus staring back at me from inside a shop window. This life-size work, probably 20 feet by 20 feet end to end (about 7 *metres* long, weighing 4 tons), was all chiseled in chocolate by the extraordinary food sculptor, Patrick Roger.

Patrick Roger is another artisan that earned the MOF designation in 2000 for his gourmet creations. Le Figaro calls him "chocolate's enfant terrible." I call him the Michelangelo of chocolate. With eight shops in France and one in Belgium, Roger is famous for his unique flavor and texture combinations, as well as for his majestic food sculptures, either for display or consumption.

He sculpts in chocolate like it was marble. He's done *galliformes* (fowl), hens, Easter chickens, and cockerels; bees, hives, and honey pots; fish; the world's tallest chocolate Christmas tree; and figures such as a Columbian cocoa farmer balanced on his toes, a chocolate ballerina named Fanny, and a naked rugby player holding a strategically placed ball. He's also sculpted animals like orangutans, hippotomi, and polar bears, plus a chocolate replica of the Berlin Wall almost 50 feet long, which used nearly 2,000 pounds of chocolate.

Roger is revered as a celebrity by many, not only because of his creations, but also due to his personal style. He's handsome with longish hair and a French "scruff" that gives him that perennially unshaven look. He looks like he just rolled out of bed, pulled on his chef's coat with the blue-white-red MOF insignia collar, and stepped over to carve a bit more on his latest statuary. Reportedly he either wears white clogs or stands in his bare feet when he sculpts. He rides between his shops and laboratory on a motorcycle.

Some of Roger's flavor creations include Trinidad & Tobago (creole rum-infused chocolate), Delhi (lemon and basil), Opium (almonds and nuts), Beijing (chocolate and root ginger), Amazon (caramel and lime-infused chocolate), Katmandu (jasmine and chocolate), and Allegory (caramelized almond, orange, and grape). He searches far and wide for products that meet his exacting standards: oranges from Corsica, Hazelnuts from Piedmont, pistachios from Sicily. Or he picks ingredients from his own garden, orchards, and beehives, which are nestled behind his kitchen/laboratory located in Sceaux, a suburb of Paris. Along the walls of his shops you'll also find single-sourced chocolate bars made with only one type of bean from places like Venezuela or Morocco.

Like many French artisans, Roger has managed to work a little sex into his chocolate creations. His 2013 Valentine's heart motif featured a subtle, but very French design of an iconic lovemaking position referred to by a number. Suffice it to say, I will not elaborate further in this G-rated book. But as a therapist, I can affirm that this chocolate creation would probably close down an American See's candy shop in an instant if Grandmother See had ventured into chocolate erotica like this. Of course the French loved it. And Patrick Roger remains the *chocolatier* to see—and taste—in Paris.

Your sweet tooth will never be denied in France. Neither will you lack for the staff of life. But it's all done with an eye toward relishing the fruits of gastronomical pleasure—and what glorious fruits they are!

What do we love about all this deliciousness? David Lebovitz summed it up nicely in *The Sweet Life in Paris*:

> "It's the bakeries with their buttery croissants served oven-fresh each morning, the bountiful outdoor markets where I forage for my daily faire, the exquisite chocolate shops that still, after all these years, never stop astounding me every time I visit one, and of course, the quirky people that really make Paris such a special place."

Willpower

P aris is referred to as the City of Light.
I might also call her the City of Lite.
Lite???

Look closely at the picture above. It's a "simple" Parisian salad of French greens, *foie gras, baguette,* and *vin blanc.* And this is typical midday fare in Paris!

In a place of so much legendary cuisine, extraordinary wine, and aromatic cheeses, how can women in Paris eat like this and stay so impossibly svelte?

I've studied French women. From a distance. And up close. Many of them stroll along the ancient streets of Paris built of stones once hurled at the likes of Marie Antoinette. They stride nonchalantly down the boulevards in their sexy short skirts, patterned hosiery, and three-inch heels. But they often have delectable *baguettes* sticking out of their handbags.

I've even seen them cuing in the jewel-box *chocolatier* shops buying to-die-for-chocolates and noshing on them while they wander the shoe department of the grand department stores. During lunchtime, I've spied Parisian women fingering a Ladurée box and noshing on persimmon and tangerine *macarons* while waiting in the *métro*. I've even watched a pair of 30-ish women eat a four-course lunch in a small Marais *café*—then polish off a huge tulip bowl filled with whipped cream laced with *sauce au chocolat!*

Still, these vexatious French women remain thin, thin, thin.

How do they do it?

Fortunately for the rest of us, their secrets are trickling out. For starters, I've always considered myself to be a fairly normal-sized adult American woman size 8-10 (although true average in the U.S. is size 12-14). I hovered in my 20s around size 6, but as the decades advanced, Mother Nature (and my fondness for French food) has nudged me up to size 10 (occasionally back down to size 8). In Paris, however, I'm considered un-thin.

From my viewpoint, Parisian women under the age of 40 all seem to me to be about a size 4. (Many of them are even smaller.) In America, we might consider some of them anorexic (severely undernourished) or diagnosable with body-dysmorphic disorder (a skewed sense of body proportion that becomes an obsession). Yet these French gals live their lives fed by the milk of French cuisine and still manage to stay slender *and* healthy. In fact, according to recent statistics, France is among the top five countries with the greatest longevity for women.

But it's still a paradox.

The French have some of the most abundant sources of food and wine on the planet. As a culture, the French are all about the pleasures of cuisine—preparing, planning, consuming, and dissecting their experiences with food. They plan much of their daily lives around eating. They consume food with relish. They make the sheer art of working with food a source of lifetime pleasure and an esteemed profession.

Yet their uniquely French approach to *eating* seems to keep them slim. I've learned that the French savor, rather than devour food. They see a meal as an all-encompassing experience to be felt, rather than downed mindlessly. Their food IQ is exceptionally high—especially from the view of an American who's used to shopping at grocery stores selling bulk consumables like shrink-wrapped produce and meats or fish with marginal taste.

The French, on the other hand, have centuries of experience cultivating exquisite produce like *fruit frais* (fresh fruit) of a wide variety. They grow or purchase flavorful *légumes* (vegetables) for dishes like *ratatouille* and *crème fraîche galette* with heirloom tomatoes. They know exactly when these products are fresh and where and how to use them. Typically, they will not tolerate subpar produce; and they will be very vocal about it if they're given it.

The French have also mastered the art of using common and exotic *poissons* (fish) like sole and sea bream in world-renowned dishes like *sole meunière* and *la daurade royale*. They've perfected a multitude of exquisite French sauces like *bordelaise* and *sauce mornay*. And they're expert with *viandes* (meats) carved from every portion of the animal, including entrails, snouts, brains, and various other parts. They're probably born being able to recognize each of their 450+ varieties of cheese, many of them protected or regulated. They, of course, produce so much of the world's great wine they probably have wine molecules in their genes.

So how do these Parisian women live steeped in this food and wine culture but stay so slim and healthy?

The fact is they're disciplined. They have phenomenal willpower.

I've discovered they eat sparingly of their fabulous cuisine. Gluttony is out in France. Like French seduction, the French enjoy the chase, the preparation, the presentation, and the recap of their food experience just as much as the culmination of their efforts. Food is to be relished, not gulped. The secret of these slim French females is that they're judicious about what they actually put into their adorable mouths. If they nibble on a chocolate after lunch, they apparently forgo a course or two at a later meal. Hence, the two young women lunching near me in the Marais were content with only their *crème* and chocolate sauce sans ice cream or cake. In America, we would've been looking for the chocolate brownie under all that cream!

My fellow author and Parisian Olivier Magny (*Stuff Parisians Like*) says moderation is almost "the Parisian plague." He adds, "Excess is vulgar." Eating bits and bites is *de rigueur* in France; second helpings are not.

And these Parisian women keep moving to keep off what they *do* eat. They take the stairs, especially since elevators aren't plentiful in Paris. They race through the *métro*. They shop a little more to work off the extra calories. They have extra sex.

But one of their best-kept, stay-thin secrets is soup.

Yes, soup.

I've discovered that many nights, the French are *not* enjoying five-course dinners of *escargot*, veal *en croute, fromage,* and *tarte aux pommes*. They are, in fact, supping on soup (like the beautiful broth pictured topped with berries and *crème fraîche*).

The popularity of French onion soup is no accident. While many of us Americans think a meal of soup is a delicious, occasional alternative, the French consume several bowls of soup in a single week as part of their regular diet. Steaming broths. Soups with names like *soupe au pistou* or shrimp and lobster *bisque*. *Bouillabaisse*. *Soupe à l'ail*. *Soupe aux Châtaignés*. *Potage aux Légumes*. Purees. Bread soups. Clear soups. *Bouillon*. The list goes on and on. These soups are healthy, made fresh from in-season ingredients, usually infused with fragrant enhancements like cognac or thyme. They're delightfully filling with far fewer calories than a large meal.

Another French eating secret is portion control. French women don't get fat as Mireille Guiliano's book suggests, because they traditionally don't *eat* that much of all that heavenly fare. Portions are small. The starters are sometimes tiny little tidbits that consist of one *fromage blanc*-stuffed mushroom cap elegantly perched on a single lettuce leaf. The main course may be some delectable fish or meat served with two or three *al dente* vegetables; but I guarantee you it will not be anywhere the size of an American ponderosa steak topped with mushrooms ponied up to an Idaho spud slathered in butter and sour cream.

Dining is about subtlety in France.

French main courses often feature items like small, crisp *pomme de terre* (potatoes) or a tablespoon of *tomatoes provençal* (braised tomatoes) that sit pertly on a plate next to a filet of perfectly poached salmon with a dollop of toasted pecan butter—about 400 calories max. When the cheese course is offered, Parisian diners will slice off paper-thin nibbles from the wedges of *Camembert* and *Rocamadour*; they won't hack off hunks of cheese the size of a Twinkie to chomp on with a tanker of red wine to wash it down. And when the dessert course ultimately arrives (and it inevitably will), it may be just two elegant squares of La Maison chocolate or a small *ganache* truffle with pistachio sorbet in a tiny *tuile* (edible cookie) cup.

The secret is complex flavors, small portions, and luscious bites.

And then there's bread.

I know, I know. I suspect many Americans are like me. We see those yummy French *baguettes* and down them like manna from heaven. So how do the French avoid the bread bulge? The French do eat bread with most meals, but I notice they consume it more in nibbles and bites. Or they use it as a utensil for sopping up the elegant sauces. Again, they seem nonchalant about eating regular quantities of bread—especially perhaps because they know they'll be picking up another loaf tomorrow. Bread recipes are controlled. There's no junk. (Perhaps it doesn't even have the calories of normal American bread. Or perhaps it's just flour magic.)

But bread is often the downfall of Americans at home. Unfortunately we have a *big loaf* mentality compared to the French. In the States, we buy a hunk of bread, sometimes the size of a small watermelon, and plow through it with gusto. Parisians, on the other hand, have bread with many of their meals, but let's face it a *baguette* is long and *thin*. And tomorrow there will always be another delectable *baguette* within walking distance, so there's no need to gulp.

Traversing the streets of Paris also helps keep Parisians in shape. I once walked 77 miles in one week in Paris, according to my pedometer. And I'm not a marathoner. I was simply meandering through all the markets and wandering the streets. The next thing I knew I'd practically walked the distance from Los Angeles to San Diego. (Good shoes are a key to fun in Paris.) Many Parisians shop daily for their food—so they have to mostly walk to obtain it since parking is difficult and many Parisians often don't own a car. Though they also have *supermarchés* where they can buy any foods required, many prefer the outdoor markets sprinkled throughout Paris (and beyond) so they can get the freshest ingredients. They'll also go a distance for what they want. They're very exacting about what they buy—probably because every bite counts!

The long, charming street markets sprinkled throughout Paris, where much of the shopping is done, consist of long avenues of carts and stands (booths) brimming with fresh vegetables, *foie gras*, meats, fish, pastry, cheese, wine, fruit, and other delicacies. And when you shop these markets like a native, you'll walk off even more pounds, not just by shopping on foot, but by negotiating around the *dames âgées* (elderly ladies) and seasoned Parisians. These eagle-eyed shoppers know how to get the best produce—and they sometimes get it by cutting in front of you! (Note: Parisians know how to cut in line better than any group I've seen. They somehow think it's their birthright to go first. So hold your ground.)

Food purchasing is also a Parisian art that lends itself to healthy eating. Since the refrigerators in Paris are relatively small by American standards, the French can only buy for a day or two of meals. They therefore plan meals carefully and buy exactly the right ingredients. Ask the Parisian fruit monger for three pears to be eaten Sunday afternoon for example, and he'll magically pick the correct three from his heaping pile. Exactly at 4 pm on Sunday they'll be perfect.

There's also another very charming French food convention that keeps the calorie count down and the enjoyment level up. It's called an *amuse bouche*. Most often an *amuse bouche* is an appetizer, but it can also be used as a palette cleanser between courses. The French use these yummy tidbits as part of their dining regimen. They're eaten with reverence and pleasure. They're not gulped like a fistful of peanuts. Sometimes an *amuse bouche* is fish or cheese on a cracker or toast point. Sometimes it's sorbet or a tiny dessert to make way for the cheese course.

I have a theory, though. All these little courses do add up to something in America we tend to call "grazing." Parisian cuisine offers these little *amuse bouche* "foodlets" along with the regular individual courses. But neither the full plates or the *amuse bouche* are very large. And they're served over a few hours at a leisurely pace. This causes the stomach to fill in small increments. Each course (even the *amuse bouche*) is given ample time to be savored; there's no rush to get to the next dish. This is in contrast to the gluttonous inclination that seizes me at home whenever I'm near a salad bar.

Another way Parisians stay slim is what I call "fork aerobics." When I learned that the French seldom eat anything with their hands, I knew that fork aerobics was a secret part of the French fitness regimen. Case in point: I once sat in a restaurant on the tiny Île St.-Louis. I observed an exquisitely turned out French grandmother and her 20-something grandson methodically working their way through a burger and fries—using a fork and knife.

While my husband picked up his French sandwich in his hands and polished it off in about four chomps, this pair took more than an hour to make their meal disappear. They'd meticulously slice each fry into tiny little segments. Then they'd cut the burger, bun and all, into bite-sized bits. Between bites, they'd both put their utensils down and converse. I was enthralled by their unhurried pace: talking a little, cutting, taking a morsel of fry, sipping a bit of wine, chewing each tiny burger bite carefully, then picking up another speck of fry.

I admit I was both amazed and aghast. This was a meal many of us Americans could have wolfed down on the drive to Wal-Mart. But I admit I envy the French control—and the opportunity to savor. However, for some eating conventions, I remain thoroughly

American. I draw the line at consuming a banana with a fork and knife, for example. Apparently, the French are trained to eat bananas on a plate using cutlery. Some of them even eat half a banana and wrap up the other half for later! I have it on good authority that Parisians think individuals who pick up a banana, peel it, and gulp it down like an orangutan are a bit backward. But some things are simply meant to be finger foods in my mind. Fries are negotiable. Bananas are not.

Still, I admire the French waistline. Strangely, I too often lose a bit of weight when I'm in Paris. I doubt it has to do with my basic consumption of food, however. It may have more to do with eating better quality food—and taking my time to walk off the calories. My energy level also seems to stay up as I hike through the *métro*, wander the long museum passageways, navigate the neighborhoods, and visit all the irresistible shops. In general, the City of Light is perhaps simply conducive to living lite: Eating lite. Walking lite. Being lite (like this svelte walker I photographed near the Sorbonne). Perhaps Julia Child summed it perfectly: "You must have discipline to have fun...[but] life itself is the proper binge."

Style

"A girl should be two things: classy and fabulous."

—Coco Chanel

French culture places a high priority on outward aplomb—or at least the will to pursue it. In *La Seduction*, Elaine Sciolino clarifies: "French tolerance of judgment and commentary about people's looks is bound up with the idea of personal attractiveness as a cultivated trait...The sin is not the failure to meet a standard of perfection but the unwillingness to try." One of the ways the French enhance their attractiveness is through fashion.

There's no better place to acquire a sense of style and a fabulous wardrobe than in the fashion paradise that is Paris. In fact, the city touts itself as the shopping capital of the world. Milan and New York might quibble with that statement, but there's nothing like browsing the opulent stores of Paris to find fabulous apparel, unmatched perfume and makeup, and charming home goods.

Shopping is big business in Paris. In fact, Gustave Flaubert, the great French novelist, said, "Style is Life! It is the very lifeblood of thought!" Most tourists are familiar with the mammoth department stores (*les grands magasins*) like Printemps and Galeries Lafayette on the Right Bank, and Le Bon Marché on the Left Bank. One of my American shopping friends says Printemps is the equivalent of Nordstrom and Galeries Lafayette is similar to Macy's.

Le Bon Marché is the oldest of the great stores. It was created in 1852 by an enterprising clerk named Aristide Boucicaut. Boucicaut had the vision to take over a small establishment and create the first department store in Paris. When I initially walked around Le Bon Marché, I was struck by all the glass and open space; it seemed vaguely familiar. In fact, it was originally conceived by none other than Gustave Eiffel who later built the Eiffel Tower a few miles away. Le Bon Marché has a particularly good men's department, with a wide selection and very helpful staff.

It's hard not to be intimidated by the sheer opulence when walking into Galeries Lafayette (GL) or Printemps, however. With its splendid dome spanning the ceiling like a gem-studded canopy, entering GL is like walking into an art gallery brimming with apparel. Between these two shopping behemoths, which are within steps of each other on the Right Bank, the bounty is mind-boggling. There are more than 40 floors of tempting items spread over five different buildings. Hundreds of designers are represented. Even GL's 5,000 square meter children's department pales in comparison to its lingerie department, which houses more than 10,000 square feet of intimates sprawled across one entire floor.

Lafayette Gourmet is the food department of GL. (It's reminiscent of Harrods' Food Hall in London.) This gourmet department offers a cornucopia of gastronomical delights. Gourmet is the word here—although candies, jellies, canned goods, fresh fish and meats, cheeses, wines, liquor, cookies, pastries, and more can be found at a good price point even for those on a budget.

While the Louvre causes many visitors to wander in awe-struck quietude, the GL food halls stop them in their tracks! One of my favorite areas is the *poisson* (fish) section where the fishmongers will entertain you while they serve champagne and prepare your luncheon. One (pictured) even enjoyed chasing me around the table with a live, alien-looking crustacean the size of my shoe. And they say Parisians don't have a sense of humor!

Across the Seine on the Left Bank, Le Bon Marché also has a grand food market called *La Grande Epicerie*. It offers a mouth-watering display of foodstuffs, wines, and accompaniments—and provides places for lunch or a quick drink. (I  think the GL food halls are more fun, however.) I have a hard time getting my husband out of any of these food havens when we visit. (He gets the same look on his face when we visit Costco in the U.S., but the price tag in Paris is naturally a bit higher!)

Though shopping in *les grands magasins* can be slightly intimidating, here are a few tips for maximizing the shopping experience:

- **Go early.** Avoid the afternoons since this is when the tour buses drop their groups after they've spent the morning at the museums. If you can start in the lower floors early on, you'll either be having lunch or already browsing the top floors when the tour groups flood in. Also, the French get annoyed when tourists try to take pictures in the department stores (especially of the displays), so you'll have to pass up the opportunity or ask permission.

- **Try to speak some French when shopping in Paris even if it's simply *"Bonjour"* and *"Au Revoir."*** This will illustrate you're willing to bridge the language gap—even if your French is less than stellar. Additionally, I learned early on to have ready shopping phrases, e.g., to get another size (*"J'ai besoin d'une taille différente"*) or to ask for the specific size I think I need (*"J'ai besoin d'une taille quarante"*). I always say *"Merci"* for any little kindness.

- **Learn your European size for clothing (add 30 to your current American size for a rough equivalent).** This may vary, so be prepared to try on a few sizes until you find the right one. For shoes, this can get tricky. A 7.5-8-shoe size usually becomes a 38 in Europe, for example, but it can vary. Plan to try a few pairs until you find your fit.

- **The more high-end the store, the more likely the staff will speak English.** But knowing a little French always helps. If I'm just browsing, I've learned to answer sales staff when they ask me *"Puis-je vous aider?"* ("Can I help you?") with this phrase: *"Merci, je ne fais que regarder."* ("Thanks, I'm just looking.") Then they seem patient with my looking around until such time as I want to try something on or make a purchase.

- **Try not to touch merchandise in a Paris department store.** Many of us are used to feeling fabrics or running our hands over potential purchases in America. But this is considered *gauche* in France. Parisian sales staff likes to help you by finding out what you're looking for, then bringing it to you. However, the more youth-oriented shops or departments are an exception. There you may find tables with piles of clothes like sweaters and lingerie where the Parisian gals will be pawing through them. If they're doing it, you can too. (Taking a moment to see how the "natives" do it is probably good advice for anything you do in Paris.)

- **Make a connection.** I've found that there's a more mature sales staff in the larger stores. If I try to speak a little French with apologies (*"Mon français est très mauvais..."* "My French is very bad..."), they're much friendlier and sometimes even strike up a conversation, asking me about American things or how I like France. In the smaller boutiques, the staff is usually younger; most likely they'll speak English.

- **Get a 10% discount.** The big stores like Printemps, GL, and Le Bon Marché provide tourists with 10% discount cards. You can also get these from your hotel or the local tourist magazines. You can claim back the tax you pay if you buy enough; just claim it back at the airport. (Check for details when you arrive.)

- **Dress comfortably, shop slowly.** Take your time as you shop, but since the French shopping experience can be a bit overwhelming, save time for a refresher like coffee or lunch in one of the *cafés* in the store or nearby.

- **Don't be afraid to ask questions.** It can be confusing when things are written in French, and you feel uneasy about asking "dumb" questions of strangers. Check your ego at the door and you'll have a much better time. Don't give up—and keep a sense of humor about yourself. I once shopped for a coat in one of the *grand magasins*. I needed a larger size to ensure my sweaters would fit underneath the coat when I belted it. I hailed a shopping assistant, and as she left the dressing room, she called back with the size: 42 (12 in America). I added: *"Et une taille 44 juste au cas."* What did I care that several of the Parisian girls turned around and stared at me? I got a great coat, and the assistant was happy I bought it—no matter the size. She couldn't have been friendlier!

- **Shop the sales** *(les soldes)*. The year begins in January with a five-week long sale (!) so it's a great time to find bargains, because Paris transforms itself into a sales mecca for fashion, interior decorations, furniture, home goods, and more. It all happens again in June when the department stores often slash things 50-75%. Even the Paris Convention and Visitors Bureau gets involved in *"Soldes by Paris."* It provides shopping guides, eating sites, and transportation information to help you spend your euros.

- **Enjoy the free fashion show at GL every Friday afternoon at 3 p.m.** Held on the seventh floor in the *Salon Opéra*, an English commentary accompanies the models wearing the latest fashions. (Obtain reservations by emailing welcome@galerieslafayette.com.)

- **Don't forget BHV—short for Bazaar de L'Hôtel de Ville** (but most Parisians call it BHV). I find this Right Bank store a cross between JC Penney, Target, and Sears. Some call it "housewares heaven." It has clothing, but also tons of paraphernalia for the home like light bulbs, shower heads, hardware, shoelaces, pet accessories, silverware, and much more (plus a wine shop).

If you prefer the smaller stores in Paris, there's much to love. On the "Girl's Guide to Paris" blog, Allison Corbat writes: "A walk down the street [in Paris] is a runway experience in itself." Shopping the well-known avenues for clothing, accessories, makeup, housewares, antiques, and more is a joy, not just for the shopping, but for the people watching as well. When you stroll the shopping streets of Paris like a Parisian, you're dabbling in the French art of *lèche-vitrine*—literally "window-licking" or as we call it, window-shopping.

To me, the smaller stores and the street markets offer more opportunity to find treasures in Paris. Anchoring the boulevards or tucked into small passages, you'll find quaint shops alongside modern boutiques. Old books and post cards, handbags and shoes, linens, porcelain, and crystal, china and musical instruments, accessories, prêt à porter (off-the-rack clothing), home goods, kitchenware, wine, and foodstuffs can be found all over.

The concessions vary from high-end stores like Chanel and Cartier to moderate boutiques like Kenzo, Promod, and Longchamp (pictured). You can also find bargain basement concessions where tourist souvenirs await your purchase. Some of the luxury brands like Yves Saint Laurent, Sonia Rykiel, Lanvin, Givenchy, and Colette have recently relaunched, refitted, or added new stores in the high-end shopping areas like Rue du Faubourg-

St-Honoré and the "Golden Triangle" of Avenue Montaigne, George V, and the Champs-Élysées. The Left Bank's Saint-Germain-des-Prés area has many attractive stores from expensive to bargain basement as well.

I find that the smaller or mid-level stores offer more personalized service and more pocketbook friendly products. (If your wallet is brimming with cash however, you may want to get a personal shopper to do the legwork for you). I particularly like Comptoir des Cotonniers, which is designed for young women but also for their mothers. Other shops like my favorite scarf store Diwali can be found in multiple locations. Diwali offers dozens of reasonably priced scarves in any color imaginable. Like many of the smaller shops, they offer personalized service and a more conversational experience.

These are some key locales to consider if you want to explore the more popular shopping areas:

- **Louvre-Tuileries and Faubourg Saint-Honoré.** Here you'll find fabulous stores along these famous streets like Versace, Hermès, Guerlain, and Yves Saint Laurent. There are also trendy concept stores like Colette, and elegant jewelry stores and perfumeries like Swarovski and Detaille 1905. I once watched a herd of people whipping around the Colette store late one evening on Rue Saint-Honoré. At first I thought it was a rabid shopping crowd, but when I checked my watch, I realized it was nearly midnight. This was no sale. Apparently the staff was completely redoing the merchandise and displays. By morning, the shop was completely transformed. When I walked by it again on my way to breakfast, there was no sign that the fashion elves had even been there!

The classic French style that's often emulated in the fashion magazines is called BCBG (*bon chic bon genre*). BCBG style is seen throughout Paris but particularly in this shopping locale, as well as in the Right Bank's 16th arrondissement and the Neuilly area. This look starts with the LBD (little black dress), then extends to the classic suits  (skirted and pants), elegant white shirts, scarves, sculpted hairdos, expensive shoes and purses, and time-honored jewelry styles. The BCBG look incorporates the styles of Spain (which is why ZARA is now a popular Spanish chain store in Paris), Italy, London, and New York, but the French BCBG woman will never stray far from her classic roots.

- **Avenue Montaigne, Avenue George V, and Avenue des Champs-Élysée ("the Golden Triangle").** The Champs Élysée area offers everything from the sublime to the tacky since it's become such a tourist mecca. (I try to avoid it except off-season due to the carbon monoxide, throngs of tourists, and the sheer density of mega stores like Virgin.) Avenue Montaigne is a wonderful, fairly quiet street to shop and gaze at Parisians shopping. It's also the locale of one of my favorite French movies, *Avenue Montaigne*. Avenue George V, a few streets over, is a feast for the eyes; it even provided one of the locales for the movie *French Kiss*. During the holiday season (the middle of November to January), the Christmas market opens in stalls along the Champs Élysée offering reasonably-priced Christmas finds—a wonderful change from the overwrought shopping that's normal the rest of the year.

- **Saint-Germain-des-Prés, Rue du Bac, and the Left Bank** near the Sorbonne is a terrific, lower-priced area to shop. Inès de al Fressange, style icon and author of *Paris Chic*, says:

> "Vive la Rive Gauche! Left Bank Parisian style travels well, and stands out in a crowd. The Left Bank Parisian stalks the streets of Saint-Germain-des Près, steering clear of anything bling. Never look rich—glitter and logos are not her thing. A true Parisian is not looking to snag a billionaire husband. She is uninterested in spending for its own sake and sporting the labels to show for it. She seeks chic, and demands quality. Her definition of luxury? A brand that guarantees good taste, rather than an all-too obvious price tag."

La branchée points to the Left Bank, Saint-Germain style preferred by trendy students and artists. This style is also called *le look intello*. It often features black. It shows up in long, sturdy coats, leather jackets, dramatic hair, heavy shoes, and general fashion nonchalance that's anything but. I like shopping around these student areas because the styles are youthful, less expensive, and fresh. I once found a fabulous cream-colored lace jacket in a boutique near the American University in Paris. It was cute, close-cut, and chic—but made in Italy! Often preferred by the *bobos* (*bourgeois bohemians* or "yuppies"), you'll find clothes by Sonia Rykiel or Paco Rabanne, among others, rare books at Rue

Saint-Andre des Arts and Shakespeare and Company, along with reasonably-priced clothing at Etam, H&M, Zadig & Voltaire, and many others. Black is the color of chic in Paris as everyone knows (although splashes of color do pop up.) Though this black and white photo of art students sketching in the Louvre looks like everyone is dressed in black, the color version looks exactly the same! They're indeed all wearing black jackets, black tops, black pants, and black shoes. *Le look intello* at its finest.

- **Forum des Halles, Rue de Rivoli, and Rue Montorgueil.** Les Halles is an extensive glass arcade that replaced the old fruit and vegetable market in 1979 amid much controversy.  Now, the Forum houses a movie theatre, a swimming pool, chic shops, and various megastores in a rather strange glass arcade that looks like something out of Tomorrowland Disney. Leaving Les Halles, you can walk the charming Rue de Rivoli that borders the Louvre and features stunning shops, touristy boutiques, and renowned establishments like Angelina's Teashop where the most divine hot chocolate in Paris is served. (Note: Angelina's now has a *café* location inside the Louvre, so bypass all the other marginal Louvre eateries and make a beeline for your mouthwatering cup of *chocolat chaud* at the *Café Richelieu.*) Rue Montorgueil is a long market street with darling shops offering cheese, wine, fresh food, meats, sweets, and assorted other shopping treasures.

L'avant garde style refers to the cutting-edge shoppers in  these areas who trend toward excess. John Galliano, known as the *enfant terrible* of French fashion, leads the pack here. Wandering around the Marais, the Bastille, and the Les Halles area, you'll see the daring colors, avant-garde outfits, highest heeled shoes, feathers, wild hairdos, and other attention-grabbing embellishments worn by women who want to be noticed.

- **The Marais.** The site of the Place des Vosges where the royals of the 17th century lived, this area was almost abandoned during the French Revolution. It's now been lovingly revitalized and is one of the trendiest areas in Paris. Many fine mansions, museums, charming *cafés*, art galleries, and boutiques share space with some of the most revered artisans of Paris, as well as a multitude of ethnic groups. Well known for the wonderful Carnavalet Museum, the Little Red Wheelbarrow (a charming bookstore catering to locals and Anglos), and the Opéra National de Paris Bastille, shopping is fun and eclectic, especially for antiques and unique gifts.

- **Île de la Cité and Île St-Louis.** Home to Notre Dame, Sainte Chapelle, and a colorful bird and flower market, these two connecting islands in the middle of the Seine are not only the birthplace of Paris, but they're also a magnet for shoppers. Famous for beautiful little shops and *cafés*, the best ice cream in Paris is also located here at Berthillon. The abundance of movie stars and wealthy folk living here lends additional luster to the island mystique. I especially love Île St.-Louis, which many tourists never find since they stop at Notre Dame and don't go any further. The quaint shops and elegant *cafés* offer a haven for thoughtful browsing and quiet dining. Cap it all off with a dish or cone of Berthillon's *crème glacée*, and you'll think you've died and gone to French heaven. Quirky note: Berthillon is closed during August (peak ice cream time) because the staff is all on holiday! The good news is that several other establishments sell the Bertillon brand while the core stores are shuttered. So French!

- **La Galérie du Carrousel du Louvre.** Situated under the Louvre to the west, you might miss this underground extravaganza where you can buy Louvre-inspired gifts, last minute finds and clothing, and even Starbuck's coffee. Entry to the Louvre is not required to access this elegant mini mall under the Tuileries.

- **Le Covered Passages.** These charming, enclosed passages sprinkled all around Paris feature a variety of establishments and *cafés* nestled in glass-covered malls. Safe from the elements, they provide charming venues for browsing unique Parisian goods, enjoying *café* life, and people watching. Passage Jouffroy, Galerie Vivienne, Passage des Panoramas, and Passage Verdeau are some delightful examples. Particularly fun is the Passage des Princes in the 2nd arrondissement, linking Boulevard des Italiens with Rue de Richelieu, which is filled with colorful toy stores.

- **Flea Markets.** If you really want a taste of down-to-earth Paris, try browsing the sprawling flea market at Marché aux Puces de Clignancourt. One of my friends says Paris flea markets are filled with "French junk," but one person's junk could be another person's Renoir. Also try the street markets where all kinds of French cast-offs, knock-offs, and bussed-in paraphernalia are available.

- **Lingerie Shops.** Lovely little lingerie shops are found all over Paris—but they're in a class by themselves. According to the French way of life, lingerie is a foundational part of the French sexual consciousness, and that's why there's practically a lingerie shop on every street. According to a recent poll, 91% of French women and 83% of French men even say lingerie is "very important to life."

Today's French consumers spend about 13 billion euros annually on lingerie. The French woman spends about 20% of her entire fashion budget on her undergarments. The well-known lingerie purveyors in Paris include Chantelle (sold in 50 countries), Aubade, Carine Gilson, La Perla, Cadolle (yes, the Cadolle who invented the bra in 1889), Princess Tam Tam, and Eres. Their lingerie collections are made from satin, silk, chantilly lace, tulle, chiffon, floral embroidery, cotton, fine ribbon, sometimes polyester, and often industrial strength elastic. The bras are structural works of

art, maximizing the *décolletage* and made from a delicious variety of rainbow colors, as well as black, cream, and red.

"There is a strong corsetry tradition and savoir faire in France," explains Valérie Charier, editor of *Créations Lingerie*, the reference magazine for lingerie professionals. "Technique and fit are very important," she adds, "but so is design. Style and comfort are synonymous." Today, French lingerie—which every French girl knows must be matching—has expanded to also include a variety of products: bralettes (sleeved confections), thongs, bodysuits, chemises, bustiers, camisoles, garters, garter belts, waist cinchers, body shapers, T-shirt bras, demi bras, push up bras, plunging bras, unlined or underwire bras, triangle bras, briefs, garter belts, and tangas, a kind of thong brief.

Many of the styles from Chantelle take their names from famous Paris landmarks: Orsay, Vendôme, Tuileries, Bastille, Pont Neuf, and Saint Honoré. La Perla has every imaginable type of lingerie—including swimsuits. Chantal Thomass, called the "queen of French lingerie," is a firm believer in partial concealment as erotic. Her motto is "hide to show better." Interestingly, the Chantal Thomass adverts and websites show most of the models in pairs or groups, frolicking in their lacy lingerie doing campy things like studying each other's derrieres, walking in the park with parasols, or feeding each other.

One of the most elegant lingerie stores in Paris is Carine Gilson Lingerie Couture. Gilson's apparel is gorgeously feminine and very expensive. It was featured in the most recent James Bond movie, *Skyfall*, where Berenice Marlohe is seen cavorting with Bond in her beautiful Carine Gilson ensembles.

Some of the famous French lingerie makers are not just designing beautiful undergarments anymore. They also offer an *entre* into the world of seduction. Aubade's website, for example, features lessons in "seductions," which appear to be pictures of their products in seductive poses—sort of like a primer in sexual posing. (There's probably more detail available, but I chose not to join their Facebook community to access the "Forbidden Lessons," whatever those are!)

Chantal Thomass's white interior shops are trimmed in colors, fantasy photos, and designs. The catalogs are playful, with models in their bow-trimmed confections popping out of bed, sitting on cars, peeking around palm trees, playing ukuleles, and in general having a naughtily good time in their "smalls," as the British would say. They remind me a lot of singer Katy Perry's lollypop naughtiness.

Eres is known for swimsuits, but decided to launch into lingerie. On their website, eresparis.com, you can find a beautiful video showing the techniques of creating lace patterns for lingerie, how the stitching is done, and how the designers fit directly to the body and more; it's sublime and beautifully tasteful.

Princess Tam Tam is for the younger set that likes the charming feel of the 1950 retro look. In the bright stores that remind me of a Victoria's Secret in America, the fun, inexpensive collections are affordable for any pocketbook. Some of the cutest designs feature high waist culottes, dainty boxers, and pointy bras in bright colors or graphic prints.

Last there is Sabbia Rosa, the lingerie connoisseur's main stop. Sabbia Rosa has a sumptuous pale green shop in Saint-Germain-des Prés. Stop by and you may see a movie star or two. The ensembles are lush and romantic.

Ultimately, you'll find plenty to buy and cherish in Paris—no matter your budget! And remember the words of Yves Saint Laurent:

"Nothing is more beautiful than a naked body. The most beautiful clothes that can dress a woman are the arms of the man she loves. But for those who haven't had the fortune of finding this happiness, I am there."

Savvy

"What is the magic of [French] markets? Above all, it's the opportunity to observe a social experience that is quintessentially French and independent of class. In the markets, real people fill real needs for food, clothing, tools, household goods—sustenance for the body—but also search for books, stamps, letters, and historical artifacts that nurture the mind and the soul."

—Dixon and Ruthanne Long, *Markets of Paris*

Wandering along Rue du Cherche-Midi one bright Sunday morning on the Left Bank, I popped out onto Boulevard Raspail and saw one of the most captivating sites in Paris: Marché Raspail. The Raspail Market, close to Le Bon Marché (the grand department store) and just down from the Saint-Germain-des-Prés area, is one of Paris's most appealing open-air markets. It features fresh fish from Normandy and

Brittany, hearty meats (including snouts, heads, ears, organs, and entrails), farmhouse cheeses, eggs of all varieties, mouth-watering poultry, aromatic breads and pastries, eye-popping fruit, scrumptious vegetables, a mélange of spices and honey, dazzling French linens, blooming flowers, and a mindboggling assortment of other goods for home and body. On Sundays, Raspail even offers *biologique* products only—no pesticides.

Behind a large stand, a robust French man in a jaunty hat with a purple scarf tied fetchingly around his neck beckoned me over. "Mr. Foie Gras" as I've named him, pointed to his splendid array of goose and duck products: *foie gras, pâté, mousse, foie gras entier* (whole livers), and more. Mr. Foie Gras expounded on the delights of his appetizing goods, and with a flourish, offered me several generous tastes on crusty bits of fresh *baguette*. (There's a French law permitting customers to sample food before buying it, by the way, so I took full advantage.) Aware of the controversy surrounding his beloved products (especially in America), Mr. Foie Gras was nevertheless delighted to provide samples and commentary about one of the much-loved gastronomical delicacies of France. For some, the smooth liver paste on a toast point is heaven in the mouth. For others, the sight of a morsel of force-fed goose liver is completely repugnant. Of course, Mr. Foie Gras (pictured) was in the first camp. He told me he'd been selling his delicacies for decades, and I con-

fess I was bowled over by his undeniable salesmanship. I came home with several cans. (I noticed the airport inspectors in Charles de Gaulle eyeing them longingly in my carry-on bag.)

Raspail Market is just one of the more than 60 *marchés* in Paris. Each is located in a different area of the city, and most are open several times a week. These quintessentially French markets provide venues for buying fresh goods at great prices—and give tourist shoppers a chance to buy like savvy Parisians. There are also 13 covered food markets in Paris, as well as various shopping streets like Rue Montorgueil and Rue Cler, in addition to the pop-up stalls pushed out on the sidewalks. All provide memorable venues for buying delightful products in a non-supermarket setting.

Paris is also renowned for its superb antique markets, as well as its bargain flea markets and consortiums for stamps, prints, leather, used books and photographs, appliances, bric-a-brac, tools, and many other items. You can find these retail sites all over Paris and its environs. Paris is simply a buyer's paradise for almost anything desired. Whether you have two euros in your pocket or $20,000—you can always find a bargain that will delight you.

Paris markets are, in fact, an ancient institution of public commerce. They date back to the 5th century when the Lutetians (early Parisians) first started holding open-air markets on the Île de la Cité to buy and sell goods and share community information. Today, many of the older French citizens do their primary shopping here. The younger generations tend to visit the larger supermarkets for staples, but many of them also love to wander through the weekend markets smelling the aromas of fresh-from-the-earth products and enjoying the pick of the market for special occasions and sumptuous dinners.

Visitors who roam through the picturesque French markets brimming with locals will see that sophisticated Paris fades—and village life emerges. You'll see fishmongers debating Parisian wives on the best catch of the day. You'll watch the cheese sellers slice off bits of *Comté* or *Camembert* and smile as the creamy goodness hits the taster's tongue in a rush of pleasure. The aroma of roasting chickens on spits and the sight of their succulent drippings cascading down onto creamy new potatoes will make you long for dinner right then and there.

You'll even hear the whimsical sounds of birds singing—especially if you visit the Marché aux Fleurs et aux Oiseaux on the Île de la Cité on Sundays. Here you'll experience the Parisian pleasure of buying fresh orchids or roses to take home to your domicile or secure an exquisite French tablecloth in Provençal blue or yellow to keep forever. A special delight is buying oysters in season—they're tasty and fresh; sprinkle some lemon on a tray of *belons* and you'll be eating like a true Parisian since more oysters are consumed per Parisian than anywhere else in the world!

Abundance is the watchword of these markets. But the French are also health conscious and insistent on natural sourcing. Three of the Paris markets are designated *marchés biologiques*. These are the Raspail Market previously mentioned (6th arrondissement), the Batignolles Market (8th arrondissement), and the Brancusi Market (14th arrondissement). All the other markets offer fresh produce, but non-organic products are also permitted. Food controls are strict in France; however, the quality of the products is assured. Many of the stall staff drives hundreds of miles to sell their wares—some even come from Italy!

To me, the markets are as psychologically bountiful as they are gastronomically rich. Shopping the markets like a Parisian highlights yet another beguiling example of how the French are formal but informal, very old and yet very new, frivolous but down to earth. You can walk down Rue Saint-Honoré and be wowed by the high-heeled ladies in their latest haute couture, for example. But one block over, the owner of a *boucherie* will be showing someone a selection of pig snouts, ready for cooking in a pan of duck fat (and he'll tell you how to cook it too). Haute couture may appeal to a

Parisian's façade—but it's the quality French produce that beguiles a Parisian's belly.

One of the things I enjoy about the street markets is their common appeal. I can talk with the local tradespeople and find out a lot about why the French feel quality and natural products are so important—and why they appreciate a foreigner who does too. When I shop for a cluster of cherry tomatoes or a jar of local preserves, the cultural barrier disappears. I'm just an appreciative consumer who values the tradesmen's abundance—and the tradesmen know it.

Julia Child, the famous chef who popularized French cuisine in America, loved shopping at the *marchés*. She relished chatting with tradesmen, examining poultry, sampling vegetables, squeezing fruit, and discussing food preparation. In *My Life in France*, she discusses the psychology of dealing with the market proprietors:

"Indeed, shopping for food in Paris was a life-changing experience for me. It was through my daily excursions to my local marketplace on La Rue de Bourgogne, or to the bigger one on la Rue Cler, or, best of all, into the organized chaos of Les Halles—the famous marketplace in central Paris—that I learned one of the most important lessons of life: the value of *les human relations*.

The French are very sensitive to personal dynamics, and they believe that you must earn your rewards. If a tourist enters a food stall thinking he's going to be cheated, the salesman will sense this and obligingly cheat him. But if the Frenchman senses that a visitor is delighted to be in his store, and takes a genuine interest in what is for sale, then he'll just open up like a flower. The Parisian grocers insisted that I interact with them personally: if I wasn't willing to *take the time* to get to know them and their wares, then I would not go home with the freshest legumes or cuts of meat in my basket. They certainly made me work for my supper—but, oh, what suppers!"

Everyone seems to enjoy the *marchés* in Paris. Even sunglass wearing Parisian bobos (wealthy, upwardly mobile bohemian bourgeois) show up to partake of the fun. In the words of the droll Olivier Magny in *Stuff Parisians Like*: "Parisians are just too cool to go to *le marché* for strict grocery shopping purposes. How common. They go to *le marché* for the vibe. Sure they shop a little, but they're primarily there for the quaint atmosphere."

Of course tourists are there for all those reasons. And it's all the better if you've got a fridge in your hotel room or apartment so you can shop for goodies and stow them for munching during your stay. One of my favorite things to do in Paris is to pick up a great, but modest, bottle of French wine, buy a crunchy-to-the-touch-but-tender-in-the-middle *baguette*, and some ripe cheese, then spread it all out on the living room or balcony table and have dinner "at home" the Parisian way. We once had a funky apartment on a street near the Ritz Hotel that overlooked an office building about 70 feet away. We could look down out of the living room window while we noshed on our bread and cheese and watch the French business people working. *Superbe!*

Many Paris visitors have taken to renting apartments just so they can have the opportunity to shop the markets and dine *alfresco*. And what could be better than dipping into a lovely bowl of fresh French strawberries garnished with a dollop of *crème fraîche* while you pop your feet up on your own couch and sip a glass of *Sancerre*?

If you want to pick a place to stay in Paris that's near the local markets, you may want to get a copy of the indispensable guide to Parisian *marchés* titled *Markets of Paris* by Dixon and Ruthanne Long. This compact little book with gorgeous photos details some 70 open-air food markets, 10 covered markets, and a dozen or so market streets with sidewalk stalls. The authors also include markets for antiques and collectibles, stamps, flowers, arts and crafts, fabrics, books, and other paper items. Identified by location and *métro* stop, the reference is concise yet detailed, saving readers tons of legwork. And you can situate your hotel or apartment near one of the markets for convenience.

For a very authentic market experience (even if it's just to taste the wares of the vendors like the Jambon Man here), go to the *Marché Bastille*. The Bastille Market is located in the 11th arrondissement and it's one of the oldest markets in Paris. Both  splendid and historic, it sits within a tennis ball's throw of the place where the angry citizenry tore down the Bastille prison during the French Revolution in 1789. Today, it offers goods to a distinctly democratic cross-section of shoppers, foreign and domestic. Walking along the narrow row of stalls, the ground seems ancient to me somehow. The air is filled with a heady mix of florals, cooking meats, soaps, perfumes, spices, and cobblestone dust; it makes me almost feel like I'm in a bazaar in Turkey. The same wonderful French cheeses, fruits, vegetables, and meats are there as at the many other markets—but there's a cadre of down-to-earth shoppers coursing through the stalls like no other.

This is serious shopping.

I see few bobos and tourists at Bastille—but lots of savvy Parisians in line for their favorite poultry, cheeses, or fish as if their week depended on it. I learned to judge from the lines which stalls were the best. Interestingly, you can see two cheese stalls within 50 feet of each other. One has a long line of people; the other has a few stragglers. It doesn't take much intelligence to discern from which one people should buy their precious *fromage*. In fact, a lot of these people have been buying from the same stalls, week after week, for years. They know the sellers—and the sellers often know what the buyers want. A vegetable vendor will set aside two bunches of fresh asparagus for Madame Puce, for example, because she eats it every week in season. Another seller will save back a basket of mussels and fish parts for Monsieur Durand because he always cooks a fish stew on Fridays.

The locals are choosy and knowledgeable. They're exacting about which pieces of fruit or which specific hare or duck or hunk of cheese they want to purchase. (These Parisian shoppers won't buy rabbits or fowl without heads on, for example; they want to be certain what they're buying, and no headless squirrel is going to pass for a smallish rabbit!) Both seller and buyer know they must match quality and price. When both agree, there are smiles—but at the end of the purchase only.

Beware the French temper if buyer and seller don't agree. I once witnessed a testy French woman and a fishmonger arguing about how fresh his sea bass was. He offered a price; she said *non*. She commented that his inedible fish was not worth the price, and he defended. Back and forth they went. As their voices escalated, their French sped up, so it was impossible for me to keep up with what was really being said. However, the woman would not back down, and soon they drew a crowd. Ultimately, I watched the fish man reach behind him and lift some very fresh sea bass from a large bucket that was more to her liking. They haggled a bit longer, but finally agreed on a price. She took her prize, which the vendor had carefully wrapped in paper. She placed it in her little wire basket with wheels that was already stuffed with cheeses, leafy vegetables, and a couple of bottles of wine. Then she went trundling off. I looked to back at the fishmonger and saw him wipe his brow, then sneak a sip of red wine. Serious shopping indeed!

Some visitors in Paris, however, prefer the more casual, self-contained store atmosphere of the pedestrian shopping streets like Rue Montorgueil and Rue Cler. The Rue Montorgueil in the 2nd arrondissement on the Right Bank is one of Paris's most renowned shopping streets. Although it was once full of homeless beggars, prostitutes, and courtesans catering to the upper classes, Louis XIV wanted the area revitalized. Ultimately, Baron Haussmann redesigned it during his sweeping renovations of Paris. Now, Rue Montorgueil is a tidy, family-friendly shopping locale.

I was astounded to see the picturesque Rue Montorgueil the first time I popped off the *métro*. To me, it looked a lot like a shopping street in California, with pert little shops, artistic signage, white marble sidewalks, and handsome window displays. The wares sit inside discreet little shops with glass windows and glass cases. Each site is brimming with appealing produce: butcher shops have packaged or fresh meats and game, as well as poultry; bakeries have specialty breads and pastries with slices of luscious *mille-feuille, tarte Tatin, brioche perdue*, pastry puffs with chocolate sauce, or *macarons*; and of course there are gorgeous wine and cheese shops. Montorgueil also has a locksmith, a shoemaker, a laundry, and a dry cleaner, plus several picturesque *cafés* for resting your tired shopping feet and enjoying a *café crème*. (Be warned, however. There are still some ladies-of-the-evening that appear in the doorways after dusk. Do your shopping while the sun is up—depending on what you're buying.)

Across town, the shopping street of Rue Cler is located a few blocks from the Eiffel Tower and Les Invalides in the

7th district on the Left Bank. Rue Cler runs through the middle of a very desirable residential area of Paris. It caters to a discerning, affluent clientele. With its small, family-oriented shops that open every day of the week, plus Saturday and Sunday mornings from 8 a.m. to noon, it's an upscale shopping bonanza where clientele can get most anything they need for home and hearth.

Or you can just sit in the charming Café du Marche for an aperitif or Le Petit Cler for some scrumptious Berthillon ice cream. The marble pavers along the streets are immaculate—and the well-dressed shoppers wandering along on a Saturday are a boon for people-watchers (and photographers). However, do things the French way or you'll get on the bad side of the proprietor of Le Petit Cler like I did one year.

Being a somewhat pushy (and ignorant) American, I was strolling along Rue Cler for the first time. Suddenly I saw an available table right at the front of Le Petite Cler *café* (pictured) in full view of the street. Since I saw no discernible line for tables, my companion and I plopped ourselves down at said table instead of going inside to the *maître de* stand to ask permission. A French woman two tables back immediately got up, scowled at us, and then headed for the *maître de*, chatting on her phone. Within seconds, he appeared to

tell us we could not just sit down at that table—we had to reserve the table a week in advance, *sil vous plait Madame*. Sheepishly, we slunk out. But we learned a good lesson that day: do it the French way or you'll find yourself in big Parisian trouble. I still like the *café*, however, and I'd recommend it any time—provided you get a reservation first!

Another charming but bohemian area for open-air shopping is along the Seine River where book, postcard, and graphic art vendors called *Les Bouquinistes* sell their wares. They've existed since the 1500s, and they're still selling their goods from big green boxes hung along the walkways. "A casual passerby might take this for a market of the mundane," say Long and Long in *Markets of Paris*, "but a closer inspection reveals everything from the ponderous to the arcane, from the titillating to the outrageous." Shoppers can find magazines, old and new postcards, rare botanical prints, early editions of books, old menus, blank menus for dinner parties, tourist paraphernalia, and historic advertising signs called *metals* for everything from Coca-Cola to Camel cigarettes.

In *Midnight in Paris*, Woody Allen even has his main character, Gil, wander along *Les Bouquinistes* until he finds a worn journal. In it, he happens upon a few words from a mysterious woman that helps him make some decisions about his love life. (By the way, for a wonderful article on the Paris places Woody Allen selected for *Midnight in Paris* check out http://www.parisperfect.com/blog/tag/midnight-in-paris. You'll see stills of the various sites like the Louvre, the Rodin Museum, L'Orangerie where Monet's Water Lilies are installed, and the Hôtel le Bristol where the characters reside. The comical but poignant story is especially charming since Paris and its environs sparkle in the backdrop in every scene.)

Savvy shopping at the various markets and vendor stalls in Paris takes some forethought, however. Knowing a little French helps (but it's typically not necessary since the point-smile-and-pay system still works pretty well in France). Understanding the metric denominations can help, for example, so you don't ask for a kilo of peaches instead of a half-kilo or a few pieces. Having ready cash is also helpful—and exact change is even better for moving the purchase process along (although many street vendors also take credit cards).

There are certain rules that the French observe and dynamics that tourists may want to be aware of when shopping.

- **Use cash or known credit cards.** Stop by an ATM machine if you need to get ready cash before you enter the markets. If you want to try to use a credit card, have it handy and try to use one that's readily accepted in France (e.g., American Express). <u>Important Note:</u> Go *inside* the bank to get your cash. Do not get your cash from an outside ATM machine, because that's where notorious thieves sometimes slip card reader devices into the machines to steal your card number. One of my friends had his card "used" three months after a trip to Paris, because his card number had been "stolen" from an on-the-street ATM machine. I always go inside the bank for my euros—and I've never had my cards stolen or misused.

- **Arrive early for the cream of the crop.** The most goods and best consumables are available early in the morning. Most of the older Parisian ladies hit the *marchés* around 7 or 8 am to get the best items and be home by mid-morning, so you'll have to get up early to beat them to the best of the best.

- **Arrive late for the best bargains.** Sellers will often drop their prices in the last hour or two of the markets, since they don't want to cart goods or produce home. Look for the bargains—but still be discriminating.

- **Watch out for pickpockets.** One of my family members keeps his wallet in his front pocket with his hand on it at all times. When I shop, I try to keep a little cash in the front pouch of my walking bag that I keep slung across my middle where I can see it at all times. But, I've never been robbed in Paris. When gathering up goods, keep your eye out for people brushing up against you—they may be thieves. Keep in mind that in France (versus Italy for example), people are not necessarily friendly and won't just come up to you unless they're perhaps "up to something."

- **With fresh produce, let the seller do the picking.** In America, we typically pick our own fruits and vegetables from big piles in the grocery store. In France, the vendors like to pick the fruit or vegetables for you; they'll be offended if you root around in their pyramids of produce. Tell them when you intend to use your fruits or vegetables, and they'll typically find you the very best items they can for peak readiness on the day desired.

- **If you're choosy, the sellers will respect you.** British chef Keith Floyd once remarked: "Watch a French housewife as she makes her way slowly along the loaded stalls...searching for the peak of ripeness and flavor...What you are seeing is a true artist at work, patiently assembling all the materials of her craft, just as the painter squeezes oil colors onto his palette ready to create a masterpiece. The French respect taste above all—and they like someone with high standards."

- **Leave your passport in your safe back at your hotel or apartment.** Generally you won't need your passport at a market, just cash and a credit card or two. When purchasing items, my husband and I often take turns watching the transaction until the money and goods are exchanged.

- **Negotiate if you are comfortable—you might get a bargain!** Some people actually pull out a calculator and start adding up prices saying, "128 won't work—how about 99?" Often they'll get their price.

- **Ship or carry.** Many of the larger shops will ship merchandise for you, especially if it's furniture, art, or antiques. La Poste (the equivalent of a UPS store) also has boxes available that you can purchase, fill, then hand over to them for delivery direct to your home for a nominal fee. Similar to a Fed Ex box, the La Poste boxes are very convenient—and keep you from overloading your suitcases going home. You can find La Poste locations every few blocks in Paris; your concierge, local map, or most vendors or *café* staff can help you locate one nearby if you're having trouble.

- **Enjoy the experience!** Watch until you feel comfortable, then go for it. You'll soon be dealing with the best of them!

Panache

The French tell me they can spot an American from three blocks away by one thing: our white tennis shoes. Before the influx of dark-colored European-type walking shoes (Ecco, Naot, Dansko, Rikers, etc.), many Americans didn't have a lot of choice other than bright-white athletic shoes for walking. Still, we Americans like our white even when we have other options. Walk around any major U.S. city, look down the street and you'll see white feet of all shapes and sizes trekking toward you.

Parisians on the other hand, tend to look down their noses somewhat when American tourists alight from buses and cabs dressed like they're ready for lawn tennis. Perhaps it's their practical French nature. The French have trouble understanding why tourists can't find dark shoes that blend in with the soot of ancient buildings and 500-year-old cobblestones.

Black is in in Paris. Not only is it prudent, it's fashionable as well. Right at any time of day or night, it's elegant for a monochrome look. Women wear it. Men wear it. The old and the young wear it in France.

White shoes are pretty much out in Paris with one exception: if you're a Parisian wearing pale Converse shoes, you're *très chic*. Worn with a pair of skinny jeans, the trendy Parisian overlooks the light color of his or her Converses because Parisians have made Converse hip.

Leave your bright whites at home though if you want to fit in in France. If you're proud of your chalk white American feet just as they are, ignore this. However, if you're stylish enough to at least wrap a scarf around your neck and tie it jauntily at your throat—whether you're male or female—then your feet may be overlooked. Parisians have a way of adding a scarf, or an accessory, or a bag that puts their look "together." Some call it "toss-away chic." It's some mysterious combination of knowing exactly how to maximize one's bodily assets with an intuitive sense of what looks fabulous but unfussy.

The French have *something* when it comes to fashion. Perhaps it's their slender French bodies and the way they emphasize their natural assets with a hat, belt, or scarf. Or possibly it's something they're born with, like some high-fashion nucleotide that only appears in Gallic DNA. A pin here. A petite cloche (hat) there. Some fabulous black patterned stockings. A floral sweater anchored by a Chanel belt. A short skirt and jaunty shirt tied at the waist. A pair of sunglasses worthy of Jean Paul Belmondo or Juliette Binoche.

I've spent many hours exploring Parisian department stores and the trendy shops trying to figure out how French women do it. One thing is clear: they shop well. They buy a few good pieces and very little "junk." Since most French women don't have the massive closets found in many American homes, they buy classic pieces that last a lifetime. Then, they use them in a variety of outfits with *accoutrements* like a colored scarf (last Spring the color was orange), a polka dot sweater, or a cropped tweed jacket.

If you want to emulate the Parisian look, you can get some ideas from a few elements I've spotted that can help any American take on a little of that French sheen.

- **Acquire a couple of great scarves and wear them with panache.** But look like you're familiar with them. I recall sitting on the top of one of those double-decker red buses that convey visitors around Paris. I turned around to see a group of women with their scarves flapping about behind me, obscuring their view of the monuments while rapidly acquiring a lot of lipstick stains. Do your best to manage your Parisian scarf—or it will manage you.

- **Get rid of the hoop earrings.** For some reason, Parisians don't wear them much. If they wear earrings at all, they seem to prefer the clip-on look, small studs, or classy French wires with gold flower bursts or exquisite filigree shapes. (And there's a practical reason of course. Berets, scarves, and hoops don't always play nicely together. I once had my camel beret pulled down close to my ears during a November storm as I walked along the Seine. A strong gust of wind had me frantically whipping my matching wool scarf closer around my neck. Suddenly, I realized one of my hoops had gotten hopelessly tangled between the beret and the scarf, pinning my ear down to my shoulder. Nearing Notre Dame, I wondered if passersby thought I might be a candidate for the hunchback's job. My husband's giggles didn't help much, of course. Button earrings are much easier.)

- **Don a pair of impeccable little flats**, perhaps with a buckle, bow, or polka dots à la Christian Louboutin. Wear them with a pencil skirt—or anything else you fancy. But avoid them with long, billowy peasant skirts; you'll look like a flat-footed fire hydrant in a dress.

- **Wear a low-slung belt on a pair of skinny jeans.** According to many French stylists, skinny jeans should be faded and straight. Flares, bell-bottoms, and boot cuts are apparently out. (I still wear my NYD jeans anyway, often in boot cut; but if you want to be REALLY French, straight skinny jeans are a must.) Belts add that cool factor. If you're pleasingly plump, skinny belts are better.

- **Buy a *chemise blanc* (white shirt).** This can go under any blazer, jacket, trench, or scarf. It fits with a skirt, skinny jeans, cropped pant, short or long skirt. The French like to embellish their white shirts, so you may see them with bows, pleats, collars, or collarless, and in a variety of fabrics like silk or cotton.

- **Purchase a little black dress (LBD).** When Coco Chanel whipped up the first *La Petite Robe Noir*, she had no idea she'd created the go-to uniform for elegant women everywhere. But I've discovered that in Paris, there are little black dresses and then there are just black ugly dresses. I've certainly owned my share of black dresses over the years; most of them made me look like I was on my way to a funeral. The key word in Parisian black dress elegance is *little.* These LBDs have just enough cloth to fit over each Parisian curve, but no more. They leave a little revealing skin in all the right places—the trim neck, the delicate French ears, the narrow waist, the kissable knees peeking out from the hem, and the elegant arms from which porcelain wrists extend as vessels for some fine French perfume. These LBDs are little and lithe, with just enough cloth to be sexy but not to suggest raunchy. It's a delicate balance. Frankly, I'm still shopping.

- **Procure some sexy black high heels.** Yes, I don't know either how those French girls wear those French *haut talons noirs* (black high heels) on those ancient cobblestone streets. But they seem born to be able to do it. Visit the hotels, nightclubs, wine bars, or anywhere else in Paris where there's an evening party going on (like the Louvre or the VIP rooms) and you'll see French women aloft on these sexy black stilettos in their LBDs looking completely relaxed. Especially check out Georges, the trendy restaurant at the top of the Pompidou Centre. The female servers there escort customers to their tables wearing exactly those outfits, looking like Robert Palmer girls straight out of the *Addicted to Love* video. (And don't try to take your overcoat into the main dining area. One of these lithesome ladies almost got in a fight with my husband who was trying to hang his coat over his chair; overcoats are *not* allowed in the main dining area. Very *gauche.*)

- **Acquire some black French stockings to go with those sexy black heels.** Oh, those beautiful Parisian stockings. Or lacy tights that snake up your thighs to meet your black leather skirt. Parisian girls seem to wear them no matter what the thermometer says. You'll find them everywhere. In the large department stores, the small shops, and of course in the daring lingerie boutiques that pop up frequently. And speaking of lingerie…

- **Find some gorgeous French lingerie that you can wear with secret pleasure, since most people on the street will not be privy to your acquisitions.** Of course, that's up to you. I've seen a few beautiful sweaters artfully unbuttoned in a Paris *brasserie* or wine bar in order to reveal little teasers of lace and ribbons to appreciative bystanders. These Parisian gals are no fools. But if you're like me, going into one of these infamous lingerie shops like La Perla or Chantal Thomass can be daunting. Chantal Thomass, by the way, came up with the notion of "inner wear as outer wear" and her trend shows no signs of stopping. Many American girls may be used to fine French lingerie or Victoria's Secret knock-offs. But most of the American women I know grew up around Playtex and Maidenform, whose indelicate creations were originally built more like mini-corsets than mantraps. To a Parisian, her beautifully crafted undergarments are paramount—and they must be matching. So to feel really French, acquire a lacy bustier or bra and matching panties in aqua, rose, or lavender, and you'll definitely experience what it is to be French right down to your epidermis.

- **Whatever you wear, make it fitted.** French girls wear clothes close to their bodies. Avoid baggy coats, long tunics, or big sweatshirts. In Paris, if it doesn't nip in at the waist, it better be body hugging.

- **Get a blazer**—the darker the better. They wear these to dress up jeans, or over an LBD, or a little skirt, or over their white blouses. Sometimes over a scarlet *bustière*—and nothing else. Nothing says Paris like a blazer with red lace peeking out.

- **Acquire a fitted cashmere sweater.** Cashmere next to the skin is the ultimate feel good accessory. And it always looks great—the tighter, the better.

- **Score some riding boots.** Parisian girls love them. By the way, never wear flip flops on the streets of Paris. St. Tropez maybe. Paris never.

- **Pull on a striped shirt.** Coco Chanel launched the striped shirt look when she stole it from French sailors she observed around Deauville in 1917 where she opened her first boutique. A woman is always chic in the striped look—provided it emulates the Chanel outfit of a striped shirt and solid pant. Don't try a striped shirt and matching striped pant or you could be mistaken for a jailbird.

- **Carry a large bag** (designer style, but not necessarily designer made). Ditch the fanny pack. A lot of the young women in Paris have found a way to get reasonably priced fashions at places like Etam, Mango, Sympa, and Designer Depot, so you can get your big Parisian bag without the big Parisian price tag.

- **Find a long rope of pearls.** Coco Chanel started that trend too, wrapping several strands at once around her clever neck.

- Stick a cell phone in your ear or clutch an iPad to your breast as you wait in line at La Maison du Chocolat. If you're old fashioned, carry a copy of *Le Figaro*.

- Wear a beret.

- Mess up your hair—the bed head look is very fashionable.

- Wrap yourself up in a French trench coat. I do have one of these that I bought in Paris. It's wonderfully French in that I look less like Inspector Clouseau and more like Audrey Tautou in it (or so I fancy). My sleek black trench has puffy sleeves at the shoulder and nips in at the waist. It also has an alluring black sheen that says "nighttime danger" instead of the "ready-for-camel-riding khaki" color of my previous coats.

- Splash on a special perfume that pleases you and only you. Remember that Marilyn Monroe was once asked what she wore to bed at night. Her answer: "Five drops of Chanel No. 5."

- Acquire the essential Parisian accessory: a Jack Russell terrier on a jewel encrusted leash. A poodle is okay too.

- And, finally, become a brunette (as in the photo). Astoundingly, most French girls have brown hair NOT blonde.

There's something beguiling to me about being around Paris fashion. Psychologically, it always makes me feel like dressing up, perhaps living out some kind of fantasy. I've noticed even older French women on the street dress up in Paris. They look elegant and self possessed. The wife of our B&B owner, for example, wore emerald silk culottes, matching blouse, and gold high heels as she served us coffee in the morning. She didn't even put on an apron while she washed dishes in all that silk!

Paris seems to have that sort of magic, particularly when it comes to clothes. Even my husband gets into the act. He wears his Kangol hat and Ted Baker scarf. When we go out on a coolish day, he even flips his hat on backwards like some high fashion photographer. When he flips his scarf over his shoulder as we stroll through the streets of Paris, he looks vaguely like someone who should be famous—and I notice there's a lightness in his step.

Inès de la Fressange, the 50-something Paris model, aristocrat, and fashion designer embodies all that is *Parisian chic*. In her book of the same name, she uses colorful illustrations, street photos, and snippets of fashion advice to explain the Parisian look. I love to study it. I can't look like half of it. But it's nice to fantasize that I can throw on a few French pieces and capture a little of the elegant chic of these exceptional French women.

I will never be French. But it's fun to dress that way occasionally. It's about beautiful play. Dressing up. Looking fabulous. Tapping that inner French girl (or boy) and going for it. In Paris, it seems the natural thing to do.

Vigor

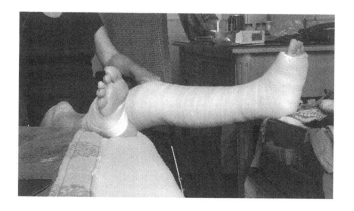

Quelle Surprise!

The last thing I expected to do was step off a stair in one of the great monuments of France and fall flat on my face. But fall I did—in front of dozens of tourists from all over the world. Worse yet, I left on a gurney surrounded by handsome French paramedics—but I was in too much pain to enjoy the experience.

When I went splat, three things soon became abundantly clear: One, my right foot had folded back on itself at the right ankle during my fall; it was now rapidly swelling to half the size of my head. Two, when my ankle gave out, I'd slammed my left leg to the ground to catch myself. It was then I'd heard an ominous crack that no human being should ever have to hear. Three, I quickly began searching the French language compartment of my muddled brain and found only two phrases: *"Aidez-moi s'il vous plaît"* ("Help me, please") and *"Merde"* ("Holy Excrement").

So began my saga back to health from an abyss of pain, prodding, and plastering with the help of the good people of France. No visitor to France can truly grasp the French lifestyle until he or she comes face-to-face with a physical disability that requires treatment through the French healthcare system. During those first harrowing moments, several local French people immediately came over to lend me support. Luckily, there's a Good Samaritan law in France. Under that law, French citizens are required to assist others in danger or distress in whatever way they can, provided it doesn't involve putting themselves at risk as well. Any French person who comes in good faith to the aid of another is automatically immune from any form of prosecution or liability in France.

While the kind locals were therefore trying to help me, the concerned museum staff also soon appeared. Within seconds, they had me propped up and began pressing ice bags to my wounds. Then came a deluge of questions:

"*Madame, ce qui s'est passé?*" ("Madame, what happened?")

"*Où avez-vous mal?*" ("Where does it hurt?")

"*Pouvez-vous marcher?*" ("Can you walk?")

Answers: "I fell down the step." "Both legs and everywhere else." "No, I'm an imbecile."

As a concerned crowd began to form around our little scene, a wonderful Italian man and his family leaned in. Luckily this compassionate man spoke Italian, French, and English so he gladly became my instant onsite translator. The French staff called out on their walkie-talkies for an ambulance, while a particular staffer I'll call Monique propped me up against her knee.

After a few moments, I began to lose consciousness from shock. My brain fogged. I vaguely wondered, *maybe this is it. Maybe I've had a heart attack too and this is my last conscious moment, here in France, surrounded by French people, lying on 500-year-old bricks that have been trod by kings.* As I slipped away, I mumbled to Monique in English, "I think I'll just go to sleep now…"

Monique listened carefully. Then she whispered into my ear as firmly as any mother could: "No, Madame, you must not go to sleep. You must stay awake. I will help you." She pulled me up straighter against her knee, and she kept me talking until the ambulance arrived. (In retrospect, it brings tears to my eyes to think of this kind young woman who helped a total stranger in a time of need. It was so soothing to have this lovely French voice cooing at me as I thought I was about to meet my Maker. But she wasn't about to let me pass to the great beyond on her watch. Part of that French stubbornness, I think.)

Soon the blare of an ambulance grew louder. Within seconds, a stretcher and five strapping *paramédicaux français* (French paramedics) came charging into the ancient chamber. They asked me a dozen more questions in French, then they finally hefted me up onto their gurney. In a whoosh, the brawny group had whisked me out of the exhibit, with my husband trailing behind like paparazzi. A few moments on a graveled walkway led us to the waiting ambulance and with one heave, I was plopped inside the vehicle (pictured). The doors banged shut. With a lurch, we headed for the nearest emergency room, sirens blaring.

It was a surreal experience, like something out of a foreign thriller. Except I definitely wasn't Angelina Jolie. I felt very vulnerable, while at the same time exhilarated to be in the middle of such a bizarre emergency. I just wish it hadn't been my own!

Within minutes, the ambulance screeched to a halt at the hospital. The paramedics flung open the doors and rolled me gently into the emergency receiving hall. Looking around, I realized I was in a holding area with a half dozen other distressed patients of varying nationalities. It looked like the television show ER, only French style. My husband went around the corner to do paperwork, while our wonderful friend and British ex-pat guide, Jeremy, who'd arrived in a separate vehicle, told me jokes about the French. (Better to laugh than cry.)

Over the next six hours, I learned some wonderful and weird things about the French healthcare system and its treatment of patients. First, there's very little privacy in a situation like this, but I did receive immediate, thoughtful care—at least at first.

Second, when all other language options fail, people seem to universally turn to Google Translate for help. Even in the ambulance, the paramedics had pulled out their cell phones and began translating my comments into French and their answers back into English for me as we consulted about my care. In the doctor's emergency care room, "Dr. M" (my wonderful *médecin*) fired up his computer and also began translating French to English and back again, as we discussed the fascinating topics of fibula fractures, *radios* (x-rays), surgery, and *basin* (bedpans).

Third, it's critically important for English speakers in these situations to know two French words: left (*gauche*) and right (*droit*). Despite my post-traumatic stupor, I was able to pull those two words out of my murky French vocabulary, or I might have ended up with a leg cast the size of a canoe on my sprained ankle and an ankle wrap on my fractured leg.

Fourth, despite my pain, I had the fascinating clinical experience of watching dozens of patients stream into a French emergency room with their broken arms, upset tummies, headaches, burns, and various other ailments. Why could I do this? Because I was parked on a gurney in the main thoroughfare outside the nine emergency cubbies in full view of everyone else straggling in with their maladies. Yes, they could see me and I could see them. We were one big infirmary.

Illness is the great equalizer in France, I've realized. French farmers. Italian cyclists. Muslim shopkeepers. British toddlers. Burned Frenchmen. Pregnant Belgians. Dizzy Germans. Greek tourists with migraines. Children of all nationalities with broken arms, sprained ankles, and bruises. And me. And we all got the same level of care—in the order we appeared.

Unfortunately, my particular fracture problem caused a huge delay. We were on hold for several hours, not because I was an American or because the system wasn't working. It was because we were unfortunately waiting for *Le Chef*. Yes, *Le Chef*. No he wasn't the guy up on the fourth floor making omelets. That's the name of the individual who's the head of the orthopedic surgery department in a French hospital. We had to wait for him to review my *radios* to see if I needed surgery! At the time of my arrival, *Le Chef* was deep in a delicate surgery somewhere, perhaps on a Tour de France celebrity with a shoulder separation. Nothing was going to happen for me until the surgery was complete and he could make a pronouncement on whether I needed surgery or I could simply get a cast and go home.

So I waited and watched.

As a psychotherapist, I'm used to seeing patients come and go, in a kind of therapeutic revolving door. But this experience in the main thoroughfare of a French hospital was truly extraordinary. Dr. M and his staff were master multi-taskers, patiently attending to each case one by one. But Dr. M remained attentive to me as well, regularly passing by me in the hallway on the way to his next patient. Over several hours, we had the same conversation several times.

(Me) *"Puis-je avoir mon plâtre maintenant?"* ("Can I have my cast now please?")

(Him) *"Non, Madame. Attendre que Le Chef."* ("Wait for the Chef.") Then he'd pat my arm and breeze by.

After a few hours, I felt bold and asked:

(Me) *"Puis-je manger quelque chose maintenant?"* ("Can I at least eat something now?")

(Him) *"Non, Madame."*

(Me) *"Puis-je boire quelque chose maintenant?"* ("Can I drink something now?")

(Him) *"Non, Madame."*

(Me) *"Un verre de vin?!"* ("At least a glass of wine?!")

(Him, laughing) *"Certainement pas!"* ("Definitely no.") Dr. M patted me once more. He was about to turn back to attend to a teenager with a sprained elbow, when he turned back to me and said impishly in perfect English: "You Americans have a phrase. Time... is...money."

He was poking fun at my American impatience. I laughed despite the pain.

"Have patience, Madam," he added in English and patted me one more time as he dashed on.

I did ask the French nurse for some pain medication at one point. Interestingly, she brought me liquid Tylenol artfully poured over a French sugar cube! It reminded of when I was a child and the nurse would hand me a tiny cup filled with a sugar cube soaked in whatever drug I was supposed to be taking. Despite the old-fashioned presentation, I gratefully took my French medication—and tried to make my sugar cube last as long as possible!

At long last, *Le Chef* emerged from his operation, studied my *radios,* and pronounced me free to be cast, without surgery. (But not before I sheepishly had to ask for the bedpan. Note to Francophiles: You haven't had the full French experience until you've heard your French physician ask you, *"Fini pipi?"* and then gingerly take your bedpan away.)

Dr. M finally wheeled me into one of the emergency cubbies and, in no time, he and his French assistant bound me up in a thigh-to-toe cast. And, after they'd wrapped my right foot in a bandage the size of a bowling ball, I finally left the hospital on a pair of elegant, pale-blue crutches.

Back at a the hotel, I had another interesting cultural experience showing the great divide between French and American treatment in certain situations. First, I was surprised by how solicitous the French hotel staff was. Gabriella, the front desk clerk, kindly brought me a silver tray of French breakfast goodies and hot coffee crowned in whipped cream while we waited for a wheelchair to arrive. She watched over me for the next hour like I was a baby chick.

Second, I also encountered another American as I sat there. About three feet from my elbow sat an American businessman, hunched over his laptop. He studied my cast and me for a moment. Then he leaned over and said:

(Him) "I'm from Chicago. Just got in this morning. That looks bad. Did you have a skiing accident?"

(Me, sorry I didn't have something more glamorous to say.) "Nope. Missed a step and went splat. Then I heard a crack—and now I've got this thing (pointing to my cast.)" I waited for the inevitable pat on the shoulder from a fellow American.

Instead, I heard this: "Well...you'll be really surprised how fast your leg atrophies under that thing. Too bad." With that, he turned back to his laptop and ignored me.

I smiled despite the fact that part of me wanted to comment on his callousness (actually, hit him over the head with one of my crutches). But I was too busy smugly munching on my croissant and expensive cheeses to bother.

Later the next day, my saintly husband wheeled me around Paris in a wheelchair. I soothed my bruised ego by buying expensive chocolates and cookies at Fauchon. The waiters around Place de Madeleine were particularly wonderful. They'd move tables aside for me so I could wheel up to the *café* table and prop up my cast. Then they'd bring me these beautiful *café Viennoise* heaping in French cream and entertain me with stories about their own mishaps. Months later, after I'd returned home and was fully recovered, I got a final bill from the French hospital for my ambulance ride, x-rays, doctor care, consultations, and cast. The total bill: 143 euros, approximately $187 (without crutches and medicine which cost me another $60 or so).

Quelle différence!

When the chips were really down, the French—and their splendid healthcare system—were there for me. And I'm not alone in this experience. Author and chef, David Lebovitz, details a similar experience in his book, *The Sweet Life in Paris*. Like me, Lebovitz had to have treatment for his leg—in his case an actual surgery:

> "When I left the clinic, I had to hobble around with a cane. Although my doctor didn't offer much of a shoulder to cry on…walking around Paris with that stick changed everything. People became incredibly courteous, and like Moses parting the Red Sea, I could part the crowds on the most jam-packed métro or markets without Parisians ramming right into me the way they usually do. *Quel Paradis!*"

One of the most interesting parts of *my* French healthcare encounter was the use of needles to convey medicine. Lebovitz and I share this unusual French experience: we were both given this huge stash of hypodermic needles to inject blood thinners into ourselves on a daily basis. In my case, the blood thinner was designed to combat bone fragments that might find their way to my heart or lungs, killing me instantly (cheery, I know). In America, we would have been given pills I think. But in France, David and I were both prescribed these gigantic, four-inch hypodermics that we were expected to inject into our bellies.

After some contemplation, I decided that after tolerating a broken leg and a sprained ankle, sticking myself in the stomach with a hypodermic seemed like no big deal. So I pulled one out, poised it over myself, and did the deed. No problem. I did this every day until I returned to the U.S. When I finally hobbled into my California orthopedic surgeon's office, I handed him what was left of my gigantic bag of hypodermics. He peered into the bag, pulled one out, and chuckled. "They wanted to be sure you wouldn't die. But you won't need these anymore. Would you like me to pitch the other 46 you have left?" "Gladly," I replied. (He also pulled out his buzz saw, and within minutes my French cast fell off like a sliced hot dog bun. I left his office in a cute little gray boot and was back walking and going to the gym within six weeks.)

Be assured, I'm now well and fit; I've even been back to France since my unfortunate fall. But I have far less fear of something awful happening to me now since I've had the pleasure of experiencing the highly rated French healthcare system. Surely its achievements contribute to the remarkable vigor and long lives of French citizens. David Lebovitz adds,

"The World Health Organization calls the French health care system, 'the best in the world,' and French people have the third-highest life expectancy on the planet (Americans are a bit further down—we're twenty-fourth). Perhaps the French live longer since they don't have to worry about medical bills, or have to cope with the stress of spending hours on the phone with their health insurance company fighting for coverage."

One other aspect of the French healthcare system that makes me feel secure: they make house calls. At my hotel in Paris, the day after my fracture, a local doctor came to draw my blood in order to test my blood platelets. As instructed, we'd simply called a number for a mobile doctor and he came and took my blood at my hotel! I got the results the next day from a Paris laboratory, and I was able to carry the data home on the plane to my American doctor. David Lebovitz echoes this experience:

"A few other advantages of the French health care system: doctors still make house calls, and each neighborhood has nurses who will give you a shot, change bandages, and remove stitches. (They make house calls, too.) Doctors give you their cell phone numbers—gladly, and you can dial SOS Médecins at any time of the day or night and they'll come racing over, within an hour, to cure what ails you. Prescriptions rarely cost more than 10 euros."

I discovered that pharmacies in France are very friendly as well. I learned about the case of an American woman, for example, who got all the way to France from Washington State when she realized she'd forgotten her thyroid medication. After obtaining a fax copy of the bottle label from a relative at home, she found that instead of seeing a local French doctor, she could simply head straight into any French pharmacy and they would supply her the medication.

When she got there, the pharmacist told her: "We can simply fill the prescription as it is written on the bottle label. You do not need to see a *médecin* (doctor) for this in France. Pharmacists here have the authority to replace forgotten medications in many instances." She got her medication right away—and it cost less than half of what it cost her at home. French pharmacists can also diagnose ailments, give advice, and often dispense medication, bypassing a doctor altogether, in some instances.

Priceonomics.com released some charts in 2013 comparing the differences between costs in American and European healthcare systems. In 2009, for example, Americans reportedly spent $7,960 per person on healthcare, while the French spent only $3,978. An angiogram in France cost $264 in 2012; in America it ran patients $2,430! An abdominal or head CT scan in France in 2012 cost about $183; Americans had to plunk down $1,670+ for the same treatment. In the same period, an MRI in France ran patients about $363, but in America it cost just under $2,871. For mothers in France, their 2012 birthing costs ran about $3,500; in America our mothers and their little bundles of joy were lucky to walk out the door for under $16,000. I could go on, but you get the idea.

Others have had the astounding French healthcare experience of low cost and exceptional care. Martin Varsavsky wrote in an April 2013 article titled "US vs. French Medical Care, My Personal Experience" on the *Huffington Post*:

"I had a 3 cm cut on my chest that urgently required stitches. I was rushed to Hopital St. Antoine [in Paris]...I was successfully treated and sent home in less than 90 minutes...they did not care if I lived in France or not, nor that I did not have any documentation on me. They treated my injury with great professionalism and sent me home...Americans spend the most on medicine but live much shorter lives than most in the developed world. They rank 48th in the world in life expectancy. France is 16th."

Visitors in France have a number of options for getting treatment. Calling 3624 in France will connect you with SOS Médecins. These kindly doctors will come to your hotel or apartment 24 hours a day in their vehicles with a full complement of medical equipment and supplies. In Paris, you'll need to say you're in department 75. This price varies from 50 to 75 euros and you pay in cash or check (in euros). You can also ask for an English-speaking doctor.

SAMU provides ambulances and other urgent medical aid services by calling 15 in Paris. Local hospitals will treat you, even if you're a walk-in. The cost may be nothing or only up to 20% of the services rendered. You can also dial 18, which is the local Paris fire department. *Les pompiers* (firemen) are trained to treat various emergencies and will coordinate emergency care and other services.

Ultimately, staying well in France is certainly a priority. But if you should find yourself in need of services, you'll find plenty of compassionate French resources to get you back on track.

Inspiration

"Paris is the kind of city butterfly catchers have trouble netting, tacking down, and studying. Like all great cities and yet unlike any other, Paris is alive and fluttering. It changes with the light, buffeted by Seine-basin breezes. This place called Paris is at once the city of literature and film, an imagined land, a distant view through shifting, misty lenses, and the leftover tang of Jean-Paul Sartre's cigarettes clinging to the mirrored walls of a Saint-Germain-des-Prés café."

—Davie Downie, *Paris, Paris: Journey into the City of Light*

There's no more beautiful sight than *La Tour Eiffel* shimmering against the nighttime sky, her Pierre Bideau lights twinkling toward space, beckoning to all, human and alien.

At her crown, a blazing searchlight sweeps across Paris, flashing a dazzling welcome.

What is it about sparkling Paris that inspires us?

Certainly there's her wonderful *panache*, her grand museums, and her fashionable citizens. There's her incomparable cuisine and legendary wines. But there are also her dubious streetwalkers, subterranean skeletons, long exhibition lines, overpriced hotels, and her dogged insistence on speaking French.

It's all part of her charisma.

Life in Paris churns in a roiling sea of humanity that both pleases and surprises. There are the exquisite little moments on a Paris avenue or in a Rue de Rivoli *café* when we glance at someone and they look back with a lingering connection. Or when we see a fabric in a shop with hues that dazzle like some forgotten royal robe of yore. Or we glimpse ourselves in a shop window and see a strange happiness emanating from a face we know but don't quite recognize. In *Paris: The Secret History*, Andrew Hussey writes:

> "Parisian mysteries appear on the surface of everyday life—the smile of a stranger on the métro, a bar you've never been to before, a visit to a forgotten part of the urban hinterland. The pleasure of the city can also be occluded, impenetrable and sometimes dangerous."

Paris is most often the idealized city of love. Her romantic *cafés* and crooked streets are places where we linger, savoring the ambience with a lover or perhaps alone, nursing an *apéritif* or *café crème*, settling in to the unhurried Parisian pace. In Paris, it's easy to be swept into her vibe. An encounter at a fountain with a Parisian who wants to take our picture makes us perhaps want to learn more about them. The random couple's lock on the Pont de

L'Archevêché Bridge piques our curiosity about what brought the sweethearts there.

Paris is also an enduring presence, weathered by the ravages of warring agendas over many centuries. Beneath her veneer of *élan*, the cracks of age peak through. And when riots erupt in the streets and angry, underemployed immigrant voices fill the air, the face of today's Paris sags under the weight of modern problems that no amount of romanticism can mask.

Still we love her. For her beauty and for her scars.

The hallowed and the profane exist side by side in the City of Light. As I walk the charming streets around St. Sulpice, for example, I'm entranced by the aged buildings and darling shops. And just when my mind is humming with the enchantments of France, I turn the corner and bump into a pair of street bums leaving their "mark" on a newly mosaicked wall. I've wandered along the Seine River, watching the golden sun dip majestically behind the Eiffel, and my then reverie is shattered by a stout woman in middle-European garb who foists a "found" gold ring on me and then demands money. It's the old bait-and-switch technique to pry cash out of tourists. (A sharp *"Vous arrêtez"* sends her quickly on her way.)

But this is all just part of the teeming inspiration we find in Paris.

"Paris seduces without mercy," Andrew Hussey proclaims. "The history of Paris is not simply a tale of princesses and kings: in some ways, it is quite the opposite. Paris is, after all, the city where, after centuries of bloody conflict, the people's revolution was invented." Paris may clothe herself in pretty petticoats, but underneath her *façade* is a rod of steel peasantry that has survived centuries of invasions—enemy, trader, and tourist—and still Paris maintains her basic nature, alluring yet mercurial.

When I go to Paris, I'm often conflicted. I don't particularly like the smoke in the *cafés* or the garbage in the streets or the thuggish energy around Les Halles. But I love long walks along the Tuileries graveled paths where I feel an awe-inspiring peacefulness. I adore the gentle Luxembourg Gardens Lake where carefree French children sail their little boats in innocent abandon. I truly enjoy the hushed environs of the saintly churches like the Basilica of the Sacré Cœur where I feel especially close to the All That Is. And I grow inspired by all the students around the Sorbonne, philosophizing, flirting, drinking, and birthing the Paris yet to be.

What I like about Paris is that life, inexorable life, undulates within and around her. I go to Paris for the experience of being in her culture, among her people. A culture that has adapted to the prevailing winds of global change, while maintaining a stubborn devotion to its unique niche in the world.

I frankly admire the way the French are a bit set in their ways. The way they attempt to keep English and computer-speak out of their language, while all around them Wi-Fi and McDo are seeping into daily French life. I empathize with their anger toward social media and *Le Facebook*, which is circumventing the old French ways of family cohesion with instant intimacy that has nothing to do with the four-hour Sunday family dinners that have fortified the French family system for generations.

Surely Parisians both love and hate their city's much admired charms. These are the people, after all, who survived the Franks, the Goths, the Brits, the Germans, the Burgandians, the royals, the Third Reich, and who now also endure the onslaught of the most insidious kind of interloper: global tourists.

I own the fact that I'm one of these modern day intruders, mining Paris's charms and perhaps, in simply observing her and recounting a bit of my life there, I infringe on her boundaries yet again. I can imagine it gets harder and harder to navigate the growing legions of tourists as you seek out your daily *baguette*. Or when you're forced to tolerate American, British, German, or Asian second-home buyers moving into the flat next door, installing satellite dishes and granite kitchens.

But the essence of Paris remains. She's a beautiful paradigm that shifts, yet maintains her core allure. Why do I say paradigm? As a psychotherapist traveler, I'm fond of many theories of psychology, among them the disciplines of Freud, Jung, Adler, Erickson, and Perls. These theories help me to contextualize the cultural and behavioral identity of a place like Paris. My favorite among them is Gestalt Theory, popularized by Fritz and Laura Perls. Gestalt Theory posits that the brain has an organizing tendency, and that the human psyche sees things as a whole before perceiving their individual parts. It also suggests that the whole is greater than the parts, but the parts are forever impacting the gestalt of the whole.

To me, Paris is her own, unique gestalt.

We all know her. I doubt there are many people on the planet who fail to "link in" to the "Paris Gestalt" when they see a photo of the one-of-a-kind Eiffel Tower, for example. Paris exists as a complete concept—a cultural, historical, and behavioral location on the planet that projects a consistent paradigm.

When we go to the City of Light, we enter the Paris Gestalt. We're treated to Paris as she exists here and now under our feet. We breathe her air. We rub elbows with her people. We have experiences good and bad. We travel home with her treasures. Perhaps we marry into one of her families. And some of us, like Princess Diana, even shed our mortal coil there. No one leaves without being touched by Paris.

When we enter the gestalt, we can try to change it to suit our cultural expectations—or simply go with the flow. We can decide to like the French—and ignore their rudeness. We can make up our minds to admire the couture—and chalk up the urine in the streets to eccentricity. We can be lured by her seductive lingerie and sophisticated ladies—and downplay any perceived wantonness. We can feast on her luscious, expensive food—and simply enjoy it.

Above all, the experience of Paris is to be *lived*. We can shop the great department stores or small shops, finding sophisticated treasures or a few homemade French goods to cherish when we return home. Among them is the famous Laguiole knife, the sinuous Occitan blade of Southern France with its handsome shaft adorned by a royal bee purchased by my ecstatic friend Roger.

If we are adventurous, we can play boule in Paris like these fellows.

We can take a cooking class and enjoy the forthrightness of French chefs. There are chefs like Damien (pictured) who are perfectly willing to dismember an entire pig for us—then demonstrate how each segment is used in fine French cuisine, entrails and all.

We can learn to make *macarons* from scratch from France's decorated pastry chefs like my friend Angelica.

We can sketch a masterpiece in a sidewalk *café*.

We can take our dog to lunch.

Or we can sit in a *café* and simply be.

And at night, we can enjoy the most magical side of Paris. When the sun sets and the street lamps come alive, Paris glistens, muting the wear of the centuries, awash in an otherworldly glow. And sometimes magic happens.

One night, my husband and I had a most amazing nighttime experience that sums up my sense of Paris as a place where dreams can happen—and the memories of a lifetime can be born. We'd been in Paris for about a week in November 2010. The air was cool and crisp; the Christmas decorations were just appearing. That Friday evening we'd dressed up in our very best—a combination of American evening clothes and French accessories, including Chanel No. 5 (on me of course).

We sauntered around the corner from our rented apartment on Rue Danielle Casanova, and headed for the Ritz (pictured) across the Place Vendôme in the center of Paris. Sports cars, limousines, taxis, and town cars sped past us; many made the U-turn and rolled up to the front

of the Ritz. Guests and tourists alighted for dinner, drinks, and perhaps a romantic rendezvous.

Our destination was the hushed and intimate Bar Vendôme. We had dinner reservations elsewhere at a medium-to-high-end restaurant in the 8th arrondissement, but we'd decided to stop in at the Ritz for a before-dinner *apéritif.* The staff seated us at a wonderful table near the garden window. It overlooked the rich mahogany and velvet furnishings of the room, as well as the grand piano. Our server brought us a pair of elegant cocktails, accompanied by warm nuts and delicate vegetables served in fine Ritz porcelain.

Soon, it was time to depart. We rose and headed to the Place Vendôme entrance. There we joined a long queue of people waiting for taxis or private cars. We slowly inched forward. I noticed that several of the couples or small groups ahead of us were dressed in blue jeans or similarly casual wear. The intimidating, but bored Ritz doorman (who reminded me a little of Daniel Craig, the latest James Bond), was hailing taxis for most of the groups.

When it finally came our turn, my dapperly dressed husband asked the doorman for a conveyance to our restaurant, whereupon he handed the doorman the name of the restaurant on a slip of Ritz paper. Suddenly the doorman's demeanor changed. He smiled and nodded to my husband while subtly appraising me as only a French man can. He tipped his hat at me and smiled.

Swiftly, he lifted his wrist walkie-talkie and began speaking to an unknown entity somewhere. We patiently waited as the doorman scanned the square. It seemed to be taking a long time. I stood there thinking the Friday night activity must be keeping the taxis very busy.

Suddenly, a sleek, chocolate-colored town car with chrome wheels grandly pulled up to the front of the hotel. With a flourish, the doorman ushered us forward and opened the door of this fabulous vehicle to seat me inside. Since I'm not a car aficionado, I had to take my cue from my husband who, by this time, had entered from the opposite side and was now seated beside me. I glanced over at him. He looked strangely intoxicated—or at least like he'd just won the lottery *and* a private jet!

I knew we were about to ride in something special. I slid my hand over the seat and felt plush leather like I'd never encountered. At the same time, I attempted to maintain some decorum, but I couldn't take my eyes off the driver with his close-cropped hair, chiseled face with French stubble, slim-cut black suit, and expensive driving gloves. He looked like someone who should be driving Nicholas Sarkozy (former French President), not a pair of Californians with a dinner reservation!

He greeted us with *"bonsoir"* in thickly accented French. Then he studied the restaurant information. I took that moment to observe the interior of the vehicle. It was beautifully outfitted with fine wood, richly carpeted floor, and soft blue accents. Within seconds we were gliding across the cobblestones along Rue Saint-Honoré past the Hôtel Le Bristol Paris. It was then I noticed a strange thing happening. At each intersection, it seemed like the other cars slowed slightly, allowing our vehicle to go first. I glanced over at my husband to see if he noticed it, but he was now looking at me like we'd just robbed Fort Knox. Finally, we arrived at our restaurant and our suave driver helped me out of the car. (I think I sniffed Dior's *Eau Sauvage* as he leaned over.)

A few moments later we were seated inside the restaurant. Suddenly, my husband burst into laughter. "What just happened?" I asked incredulously.

"Oh my god," my husband practically shouted. "Don't you realize we just rode in a $200,000 Bentley Continental with Ritz license plates??? They must have thought I was Bill Gates! The traffic practically parted to let us pass—didn't you see it?"

"I noticed," I said thoughtfully. Then I added as only a wife could, "Aren't you glad we dressed up?" My husband answered with another peal of ecstatic laughter—and it's been his favorite Paris story ever since.

Paris is indeed an effervescent butterfly. She flits through our psyches like some intoxicating creature that stays for an instant, but lives in memory for a lifetime.

Ultimately, we bring *ourselves* to this enchanting world of Paris. And Paris gifts us with all that she is, smooth and rough, glitter and rust.

What we do with those gifts is up to us.

Resources

1000 Years of Annoying the French by Stephen Clarke (see also the *Merde* series)

Accounting for Taste: The Triumph of French Cuisine by Priscilla Parkhurst Ferguson

All You Need to be Impossibly French by Helena Frith Powell

Au Contraire! Figuring out the French by Gilles Asselin and Ruth Mastron

Beaux Gestes: A Guide to French Body Talk by Laurence William Wylie

Bébé Day by Day: 100 Keys to French Parenting by Pamela Druckerman

Born to Shop Paris by Suzy Gershman

Born to Shop France by Suzy Gershman

Bringing Up Bébé (French Children Don't Throw Food) by Pamela Druckerman

Cultural Misunderstandings: The French-American Experience by Raymonde Carroll

Entre Nous: A Woman's Guide to Finding Her Inner French Girl by Debra Ollivier

French Fried by Harriet Welty Rochefort

French Kids Eat Everything by Karen le Billon

French Toast by Harriet Welty Rochefort

French Women Don't Get Fat by Mireille Guiliano

French Women for All Seasons by Mireille Guiliano

Joie de Vivre by Harriet Welty Rochefort

La Seduction: How the French Play the Game of Life by Elaine Sciolino

Le Guide Culinaire by Auguste Escoffier

Markets of Paris by Dixon and Ruthanne Long

Mastering the Art of French Cooking by Julia Child, Simone Beck, Louisette Bertholle
My Life in France by Julia Child
Paris Hangover by Kirsten Lobe
Paris in Love by Eloisa James
Paris, Paris: Journey into the City of Light by David Downie
Parisian Chic by Inès de la Fressange
Paris to the Pyrenees: A Skeptic Pilgrim Walks the Way of Saint James by David Downie
Practical Paris by Karen Henrich
Stuff Parisians Like by Olivier Magny
The Pâtisseries of Paris by Jamie Cahill
The Physiology of Taste by Anthelme Brillat-Savarin
The Sweet Life In Paris by David Lebovitz
The Wine Bible by Karen MacNeil

Acknowledgments

I'd like to thank a number of people who assisted me in writing this book. Among them are: Parker Donna Tenney for her stories about Paris; Barbara Kallir, Jim Lockard, and Debbie Smayo for their perspectives on Paris life and the French culture; Angelica Pivarunus for her effervescence in France depicted in these pages; bon vivants Gary and Maureen Beals for their international perspective; Suzanne Anzalotta for her enthusiastic support; Tom Leech for his book smarts and mentoring; worldwide travelers and all-around fun companions Jill and Roger Drexler for their willingness to love the French too; Jeremy Kolbe for his kindness and tour expertise; Ashley Regan for her editorial and developmental input; Shaun Griffen for her book savvy and natural *joie de vivre*; Andrea Glass for her editorial insights and book *élan*; Karla Olson and Lynette Smith for their invaluable consulting; Suzy Gershman and David Downie who inspired me to pen this book; John Virag, Kim Clark, and the entire Sullivan family who helped nurse me back to tip top shape; the kind people and medical staff of France who were willing to offer me the hand of friendship and empty my bedpan; my irreplaceable mother and former travel agent, Evelyn Thomsen, who instilled in me the love of travel; and finally, John Birkhead, whose patience and dedication never wavers.

About the Author

P J Adams is a practicing psychotherapist, author, and former publishing executive living in Southern California. Her previous books include the psychological thriller *Freud's Revenge* and the self-help book *Daughter Wisdom*. She stays (mostly) sane by learning French, growing tomatoes, and writing about travel, crime, relationships, and healthy living.

Made in the USA
Charleston, SC
27 September 2013